Body
Language

GEDDES&
GROSSET

Published by Geddes & Grosset, an imprint of
Children's Leisure Products Limited

© 1996 Children's Leisure Products Limited,
David Dale House, New Lanark, ML11 9DJ, Scotland

First published 1996
Reprinted 1999

ISBN 1 85534 249 9

Printed and bound in the UK

Contents

Introduction   7
What is language?   7
Nonverbal communication   8
Insight through body language   11
Interpretation is not always straightforward   14
Gestures   17

Chapter 1: Gesticulation   20
Speech and body language   20
Emphasising size   21
Cold   23
Heat   25
'Haven't a clue'   25
'Fingers crossed'   26
'Cross my heart'   28
'Touch wood'   29
Pointing   30
Finger wagging   34
Other finger gestures   35
Foot stamping   35
Foot tapping   36

Explanation and description 36
Directions 37
Involuntary gesticulation 39
Examples of gesticulation 40

Chapter 2: Voluntary Gestures **46**
Intentional emphasis 46
Rubbing the hands 48
'After you' 49
Pointing 49
Kissing the fingertips 50
Licking the lips 51
Foot stamping 51
Kicking 52
Forward sweep of the hand 52
The nose-tap 52
Holding the nose 53
Wrinkling the nose 54
Sniffing 55
Chin-stroking 56
Ear-touching 57
The speechless gesture 58
Communicating over a distance 65
Waving or drowning? – misinterpretation 68
Bridging the language gap 71
Cultural differences and misunderstandings 73
The handshake 80
The fist 83
Hand clapping 85
Nodding and shaking the head 87
Obvious gestures 90

Either voluntary or involuntary gestures 92
Putting the hand over the eyes 102

Chapter 3: Involuntary Gestures 115
Habit, convention and true self 115
What people don't tell us 116
Interpretation 117
Signals 121
Position of the head during conversation 122
Unconscious mimicking 132
Hair 132
The brow 137
Eyebrows 139
The eyes 141
Cheeks 148
Ears 149
The nose 152
The mouth 154
The lips 157
The tongue 158
The teeth 159
The chin 161
The neck 163
Shoulder shrug 166
The arms 167
Hands 175
The fingers 183
The thumb 186
Legs 190
Standing 195
Feet 197

Seeing past the imprecision   199
Involuntary gestures   200

Chapter 4: Other Body Signals   **214**
Posture   214
Walking pace   220
Standing   221
Lying down   225
Spatial zones   227
Seating arrangements   234

Introduction

What is language?

Language is the medium by which we communicate our thoughts and opinions to others and by which we give expression to our emotions. We tend to think of language purely in terms of words and sounds, and this is hardly surprising since the word 'language' is associated with the word 'tongue', an organ much used in the production of words and sounds. 'Language' comes to us through Old French from *lingua*, the Latin word for 'tongue'.

Certainly, one way of looking at language is to think of it as a human system of communication, which uses structured vocal sounds and which can be embodied in writing and print. Using this definition of language we can view it as one of the characteristics that sets us as humans apart from members of the animal kingdom. The family cat and dog may succeed very well in communicating their messages to us, but their range of miaowing and barking is simply not in the same league as the human mastery of words.

Language not only separates us from animals but separates us as humans according to the area of the world in which we live, the dialect of language we speak or our historical or ethnic influences. People who live in Spain speak Spanish, but so do people who live in other parts of the world, such as certain areas of South America that were colonised by the Spanish. These speakers of Spanish will have certain significant linguistic differences in grammar and semantics because of cultural divergence.

'Language' is a word that can be applied to any means of communication, not just the vocalisation of vocabulary with a structured system of grammar. In this sense, an animal's cries, movements and expressions are a means of communicating its needs, reactions and responses and are a form of language. Into this category comes a very important form of communication – that which is associated not with the vocal chords but with gestures and movements. This form of communication has become known as body language.

Nonverbal communication

Since, by its very nature, body language is non-verbal – although it is sometimes accompanied by speech – it is also known, particularly in more technical or more academic contexts, as nonverbal communication. Body language, or nonverbal communication, covers not only communication by bodily gestures but also includes communication by facial expression, body posture and position, and touch and bodily contact.

Body language is often more revealing than speech since it is more likely to be subconscious and so can be interpreted as a more accurate guide to the thoughts and feelings of the person in question. Often, indeed, the message conveyed by body language is in opposition to that conveyed by speech. Many of us have become used to putting on a public act to hide our true reactions, but telltale gestures or expressions can all too easily give us away.

Such a scenario is common in everyday life. For example, a member of the family unexpectedly brings home a guest for dinner. The person who is in charge of the family catering, often, even in these days of increased sexual equality, the wife or mother, is in a quandary. It is extremely likely that early training has conditioned her to be polite, and in

order to put the unexpected guest at ease she may
well utter charming and welcoming words, such as
'You're very welcome. Of course it's no trouble.
One more won't make any difference as long as you
don't mind taking pot luck,' and any other social ba-
nalities that spring to mind. Most of her mind, however, will have transferred itself to the kitchen and
be at that moment surveying the likely contents of
oven, fridge and freezer. It will be asking silent
questions such as 'Can three small chops feed
four people?' 'Can I quickly casserole the chops
and eke them out with lots of vegetables?' 'Shall I
say that I have already eaten or that I have become a
vegetarian?'

Despite the hostess's valiant verbal attempts to
disguise her true feelings, however, the unexpected
guest, if at all discerning and perceptive, is likely to
become all too aware of these through various aspects of her body language. The hostess may be
wearing a bright, if rather forced, smile, but the expression in her eyes is more difficult to control and
is a more reliable guide to her real reaction, whether
this be anger at the family member for landing her in
this particular situation or sheer fear or panic at the
difficulty of expanding the meal to accommodate
one more. The rest of her body may well give her

away also in a more subtle way. She may unconsciously give way to her anger by tapping her foot or
silently snapping her fingers, or she may betray her
nervousness or anxiety by constantly wringing her
hands or twisting a strand of hair. She may keep looking over her shoulder to where her thoughts lie and to
where the source of her anxiety is located – the kitchen.

All areas of our lives produce scenarios that mirror the one described above. People's body language
gives us a much greater and truer insight into their
state of mind, their personalities, and even their intentions, than their speech ever does. It is both interesting and useful to learn more about this form of
communication.

Insight through body language
Selling
There are some areas of life in which it is of particular value to know something about body language. It
is, for example, extremely useful for people who are
in the business of selling things to acquire some
knowledge of the subject. An acquaintanceship with
body language may well be of assistance to a salesperson who is in the course of trying to make a sale.
The salesperson can learn to analyse the reactions of
the prospective buyer early on in the selling process

so that if the potential buyer is beginning to display body language that indicates reluctance or disinclination, or even downright boredom, then the salesperson can change tack and alter the style of selling. On the other hand, if the person in the buying role is exhibiting body language that denotes great keenness and inclination to buy, then the person in the selling role will know that the selling technique is correct and he or she can go in for the kill.

Buying

Of course the selling process is very much a two-way process. A knowledge of body language will benefit the buyer as well as the seller. This will be particularly useful in situations in which the buyer is trying to get a good deal and lower the price originally proposed by the salesperson. The chances of acquiring a generous discount may well be heightened if the client can deduce how the seller feels before this is actually put into words. If the seller's body language is giving off extremely negative signals then it would be as well for the would-be buyer to reduce his or her demands so as eventually to clinch a reasonable deal. Otherwise, a determination to achieve the original price objective might result in a non-sale.

Employers

There are areas in which a knowledge of body language can pay dividends. Given the fact that it is very important for employers to appoint the right candidate for a job, the people conducting the selection interviews could well save themselves a few expensive mistakes if they learnt a bit about body language. The candidates for the job will be so anxious to get the job that they will all be careful to present only their best sides to the interviewers and to display themselves in the best possible light. This being the case, it is sometimes virtually impossible to choose among them. However, unless they are themselves schooled in the art of body language, the various candidates will give a clue to their real personalities, rather than to their carefully groomed public ones, in all kinds of subtle ways. The information that their unconscious body movements and positions can supply can certainly separate those who fulfil the requirements of the job from those who do not know.

Job candidates

Again there are two sides to the story and two sides that could benefit from a knowledge of body language. Such knowledge could benefit the candidates for a job in two ways. First, they could learn to interpret the body language of the interviewers as the interview progresses. The interviewer may have a set, frozen, encouraging smile, but his or her body language may be exhibiting decidedly negative signals. Of course it is possible that there is nothing that the hopeful candidates can do to reverse this situation, but, on the other hand, it is also possible that they could retrieve the situation with a change of tactics, were they able to come to a correct assessment of the situation. Second, although this is a more difficult scenario, some knowledge of body language may help the candidates at least to be aware of the telltale body signals that they are exhibiting to the interviewers and to try to control them. This is by no means an easy task, since it involves trying to control the unconscious. However, some awareness of the signals that are given out by one's own body can at least lead one to try to restrain these to some extent, at least for a short time.

Interpretation is not always straightforward

It would be wrong to suggest that controlling body language completely, at least for any length of time, is even possible. A major complicating factor in trying to prevent people from interpreting your real personality, attitudes and feelings through your body language is that it is not as simple as one gesture signalling one attitude or emotion. This is, indeed, not at all simple, but the situation is made considerably more complex by the fact that body signals tend not to occur singly, in isolation, but as part of a group, or cluster, of body signals, including facial expressions.

As has been mentioned above, there are various aspects of body language. The physical activity mentioned in connection with the unwilling hostess, the sales process and the interviewing process is unconscious, but not all body language is unconscious – some actions that come within its terms of reference are quite intentional. Many attitudes and emotions are conveyed to others by gestures that are executed quite deliberately by the person wishing to convey them. In this book these are described as *involuntary gestures*, as opposed to those gestures that are executed quite unconsciously, described here as *voluntary gestures*.

It should also be remembered that not all body language is executed in an atmosphere of silence. Many body signals are accompanied by speech, when these take the form of gestures that are made unconsciously. For the purposes of this book, gestures accompanied by speech have been categorised under *gesticulation*. Then we have to bear in mind that it is not only the actual words that people use that count towards our understanding of the message they are communicating but also their tone of voice.

If we think of body language at all we tend to think of it in terms of movements of the head or limbs. This is, in fact, too narrow an interpretation of the subject as not all body language relates specifically to the movement of the head or of a limb. The expression of the face and the eyes is also relevant to the study of body language. Indeed, the eyes are of paramount importance. Not only are they the mirror of all our feelings but they convey a message that is very difficult to falsify.

Other giveaways in terms of body language include body posture and body position. You can deduce a great deal about the personality and feelings of a person by observing, for example, how he or she is sitting at a desk. Is the person in question slumped over the desk with tightly folded arms or is he or she sitting back with arms folded behind the head?

Then there is the question of the physical position of one person vis-à-vis another. This has relevance, say, at a board meeting with reference to positions at a table, particularly when the table is oblong in

shape. If at all possible, it is as well to avoid si
at the narrow side of the table nearest the doo
this places you at the bottom of the heap, so to
speak. The most important person at the meeting
will almost certainly have taken the narrow side of
the table farthest from the door

Often our first introduction to nonverbal language
lies in someone's facial expression. If people are
smiling, we assume that they are happy; if they are
scowling, we assume that they are angry or dissatis-
fied; if the corners of the mouth are showing a distinct downward turn, then we assume that they are
miserable, and so on. This, however, is far from being the full story. Body language is full of complexi-
ties and subtleties. If you want to try to get to grips
with these, read on!

Of course, if you take up the study of body language, a little caution and subtlety are required. If you
stare at other people to try and get an insight into their
inner selves, or, worse still, if you start taking notes,
you are liable to be on the receiving end of one of the
more aggressive forms of body language

Gestures

When we first encounter the term body language,
the word 'gesture' readily springs to mind, simply

because that word immediately suggests to us an action carried out by a part of the body, usually one involving the arms, hands or head, which is designed to convey a message. Certainly, gestures, although they do not alone make up the whole of body language, are central to its study and form a large part of it.

'Gesture' is, however, quite a wide-ranging term, and it will be helpful when considering it in terms of body language to subdivide it into categories. For purposes of the present study, these categories are *gesticulation*, which covers those gestures used to accompany speech; *voluntary gestures*, those gestures that are used intentionally instead of speech; and *involuntary gestures*, those gestures that are used subconsciously.

The situation with regard to body language is, however, not as cut and dried as this categorisation suggests, since there is a good deal of overlap within the categories. For example, many conscious gestures can be used either with or without speech and so can be classified both as examples of gesticulation and as voluntary gestures – thus the pointing finger can speak for itself or have the backup of speech. Also, some gestures can be used either intentionally or consciously and so can be classified both as involuntary gestures and as voluntary gestures – thus the tapping foot gesture can be executed with or without the knowledge and volition of the owner of the foot. There are even gestures that are so adaptable that they qualify for inclusion in all three categories.

The relevant gesture has usually been dealt with in detail under the category in which it is used most frequently. There is a passing reference to it in the category or categories in which it can also appear.

CHAPTER 1

Gesticulation

Speech and body language

When we speak, parts of the body – apart from the obvious ones used in speech, such as lips, tongue and jaws – often play a part as well. Thus we may make use of our facial muscles and eyes, and move our heads, hands, arms and feet. To what extent we do this varies very much from person to person and possibly from one personality type to another. The degree of use of gesticulation also varies from people of one nationality to those of another. For example, the French and Italians tend to use their hands freely to give emphasis to what they are saying while members of the Oriental races tend to be much more restrained.

Many of us will have friends who seem quite incapable of saying anything without a great deal of arm-waving. They are often very expansive people who care passionately about things but are best avoided if they are behind the wheel of a car, when their steering often becomes secondary in importance to the point that they are trying to make. More reticent people, on the other hand, are apt to keep their limbs more under control since they tend to be more restrained people generally.

Gesticulation in the present context is something that we all practise regularly, whether or not we are of the expansive, arm-waving brigade, for it is being used here to denote the kind of body language that accompanies speech. Body movements and speech often complement each other to make for more satisfactory communication, and although gesticulation may be the minor partner in the relationship it is often an integral and valuable one.

Emphasising size

Gesticulation is frequently used for emphasis. For example, if you wish to convey to your listeners the fact that a certain man was exceptionally tall, you might well find yourself not only giving verbal expression to this by saying, 'He was absolutely huge!' but also find yourself resorting to gesture or gesticulation by stretching your arm heavenwards, as far as possible, often with the hand flattened and stretched out, and even sometimes standing on your toes to indicate great height.

On the other hand, if you wish to indicate degree of smallness or shortness you stretch your arm down as low as possible, again with the hand flattened and stretched out, and sometimes crouch slightly, saying something along the lines of 'The child is very small for his age. He's only this height,' or 'We planted an apple tree about three years ago but it's still tiny.'

Gesticulation can also play a part in demonstrating the narrowness or broadness of something or someone, allowing for some degree of exaggeration. Someone wishing to stress how close some newly built detached houses are to each other might hold outstretched hands only inches apart

and say, 'There's no more space than that between them.'

The act of stressing how wide or how long something is is one much ascribed to anglers. Anglers are supposedly much given to exaggerating the size of the fish they catch, or more particularly the size of the fish that they almost caught. When describing the amazing dimensions of such a fish words alone fail them, and they resort to stretching both arms as far as possible to the side, exclaiming the while, 'I'm not joking. It was this size.' Suffice to say no one really believes this, but where is the harm in a little fantasy.

Cold

Similar forms of gesticulation play a large part in everyday communication with each other and add a

little colour to it. If you have just come into a warm room from a long walk in the cold you could just make a verbal comment to this effect. However, many of us, particularly those of us who are given to a bit of theatricality, are very likely to try to impress the occupants of the room with our hardship and to seek sympathy from them by hugging ourselves tightly as well as announcing, 'Gosh, it's cold out there.' The self-hug is a common indication of cold, sometimes being accompanied by a shiver for even greater emphasis. It is one of those gestures that can be used either with speech or not, the self-hug being self-explanatory. When used without speech the gesture becomes an example of a voluntary gesture, the subject of the next chapter.

Heat

The opposite of this gesture is the hand drawn across the brow to wipe imaginary sweat from it and to indicate the great degree of heat being experienced. It can be used with or without speech and has the extra meaning of indicating that one has had some kind of narrow escape. At least in the latter case it is more commonly used without speech and has been dealt with fully in Chapter 2.

'Haven't a clue'

There are many examples of gestures that are used in tandem with speech for added emphasis. When, for example, people wish to indicate that they know absolutely nothing about the whereabouts of some-

thing or someone that is lost they say something like 'I have no idea' or 'Haven't a clue!' or 'Search me!' and fling their arms wide away from the sides of the body, as if to indicate that if you choose to search them you will find nothing on them to connect them with the lost person or thing. The origin of such open gestures lies in historical times, when the person would be holding a cloak wide to indicate the absence of a weapon, such as a dagger.

'Fingers crossed'

When someone is about to embark on some venture where a degree of luck is necessary, such as taking a driving test, sitting an exam or going for an interview for a job, well-wishers will often not

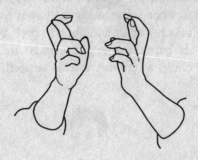

only say, 'Good luck!' but will add, 'Fingers crossed!' and frequently carry out the action that they are describing to emphasise their good wishes. They may even cross fingers on both hands in the hope of increasing the possibility of such good luck occurring. Occasionally the crossed fingers gesture is made without added speech, especially over a distance or when silence is required. For example, a driving instructor might cross his fingers at his pupil as he or she steps into the car in which the driving test is to be taken. The crossing of the fingers has religious origins since the fingers are making the sign of the crucifix, a symbol central to Christianity.

'Cross my heart'

Another example of gesticulation involving the cross is used when someone says, 'Cross my heart!' or even 'Cross my heart and hope to die!' While the statement is being made, the hands are crossed across the chest, where the heart is located. This ac-

tion is used to emphasise how truthful the person making the gesture is being. It is often used by children. For example, a little boy might say to his friend, 'I did not take your book! Cross my heart', or say to his mother, 'I will clean my room tomorrow. Cross my heart and hope to die.' Neither the gesture nor the accompanying words should be taken as gospel since they are frequently used by someone who is lying furiously and who is fervently trying to conceal the fact. Very occasionally the gesture might be made without speech, but this would probably occur in a humorous context, when someone was miming the degree of his or her honesty or reliability.

'Touch wood'

Just as we often cross our fingers as a sign that we wish for good luck, so do we often knock on something wooden in an attempt to avoid bad luck or to continue on a course of good luck. The gesture is rarely used without speech. A common context would be one in which someone would say something like, 'At least none of us has been declared redundant yet.

Body Language

Touch wood!' or 'We usually get good weather for our annual fête. Touch wood!' the speaker striking a table top, or something similar, with the fist, or simply touching it with the fingers, as he or she speaks. Nowadays it is by no means uncommon for someone to touch some kind of synthetic surface in the absence of wood. The origin of this particular instance of gesticulation lies in an old superstition, the wood from some trees, such as oak, ash, hazel and hawthorn having in early times been considered sacred. A humorous alternative to the touching or striking of a table top is the knocking of the head, a wooden head being a symbol of stupidity.

Pointing

Pointing is a common form of gesticulation. The pointing of the index finger is frequently used for emphasis. 'Would you look at that?' is much more likely to receive a response if it is accompanied by a finger pointing at the object that is arousing interest. Pointing is often used to direct someone's attention to a place, person, thing or direction. For example, someone indicating where a person lives to a companion might say, 'My brother lives over there,' and point to the relevant building. Alternatively, someone might say to a friend or colleague who cannot

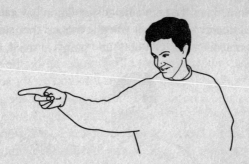

find something that is in a very obvious place, 'Your bag is over there! I can't think how you missed it!' and point to the supposedly missing object.

The pointing finger is frequently used to give emphasis to a command, as when a dog-owner points to a ball and says, 'Fetch!'

Sometimes the emphatic gesticulation has a touch of theatricality about it, as when someone shouts angrily to someone else, 'Get out!' and points at the door.

An accusation is frequently made more specific and more dramatic by the use of a pointing finger. The classic context is that of someone shouting to the police and saying, 'That's him! That's the fellow who stole my wallet.'

The accusatorial finger is, however, not always involved in procedures of a judicial nature. It is also found in more domestic settings, as when one friend points to another, exclaiming, 'It was your fault that we were late.'

Some people are more prone to the habit of pointing than others. Those of us who were taught in childhood that it is rude to point may recollect early lessons and be rather chary about resorting to pointing too readily.

Children are natural-born pointers. Before they learn to speak or when they are in the process of so learning, they quickly realise that pointing at whatever it is they want is a fairly effective way of achieving the object of their desire. Why bother to speak if you can acquire a chocolate biscuit without learning the relevant vocal sounds? So much less hassle!

Ask any parent about pointing with respect to children, and he or she is bound to come out with a heartfelt anecdote. A typical anecdote would relate to an incident in a place that was fairly full of people but also fairly quiet, such as a railway carriage or a doctor's waiting-room. Add a parent and a young child to this situation and you are more than likely to find the child getting bored and exclaiming in a piercing voice, 'Why is that lady wearing that funny hat?' or 'Look at that man's funny nose!' or any number of similar embarrassing remarks. The said remark is invariably accompanied by the stretching out of a particularly straight finger, pointed directly at the hapless victim. Parent and victim try to pretend to be invisible, hoping desperately that the earth will open up and let them slide out of sight.

The child is unrepentant. No wonder children are taught that pointing is rude.

There are cultural differences in attitudes to pointing. It may be thought to be rude to some extent in the British culture, but in Japan it is considered extremely impolite to point. When visiting Japan it is as well to remember this so as to avoid giving offence

Finger wagging

The index finger figures largely in yet another form of gesticulation. People, such as parents or teachers, are wont to indulge in finger-wagging if they are engaged in reprimanding someone. The person at the other end of the finger-wagging is often a child, but not always. Children get so used to the wagging admonitory finger accompanying such statements, as 'I've told you time and time again not to do that!' or 'Just you wait till I tell your father!' that they tend to ignore it. As we have seen, many forms of gesticulation can be used without speech, when the relevant gesture ranks under the voluntary gesture category (*see* Chapter 2). Finger-wagging, however, does not normally feature in this category, being almost always backed up by speech of some kind, even if it is just, 'Now, now!' or words to that effect.

Other finger gestures

There are other common forms of gesture involving the index finger, but most of these are usually executed without the use of speech and so are treated in the next chapter of the book, Voluntary Gestures. They include the beckoning gesture, the gesture that indicates one's presence, the gesture that indicates one of something, such as a glass of beer, is required, and a very rude gesture that translates into speech as 'Up yours!'

Kissing the fingertips as an indication of appreciation is sometimes used with speech and sometimes without. It is mostly usually a silent gesture and so is treated in Chapter 2, Voluntary Gestures.

Foot stamping

The foot is also used for emphasis in communicating feelings. Foot-stamping is very much the province of children and women of a certain temperament, and is used to indicate anger or frustration, almost always as an accompaniment to speech. A child might well scream, 'I don't want this one, I want that one!' or 'I don't want to go to nursery school. I'm not going!' while stamping a foot with great vehemence. A young woman remonstrating with her escort for being late might well stamp her foot while shrieking something along the lines of, 'How dare you be late! I've been waiting for hours!'

Foot tapping

The foot can also be used in other forms of body language. Some of these, such as foot-tapping to indicate impatience or anger, are less likely to be accompanied by a few well-chosen words, leaving the gesture to speak for itself. This being the case, foot-tapping is covered in Chapter 2, Voluntary Gestures. Since people can indulge in foot-tapping without being aware of it, the action also merits a mention in Chapter 3, Involuntary Gestures.

Explanation and description

As has been indicated above, the marriage of speech and gesture is frequently used for emphasis, but it is also often used for illustratory or explanatory purposes. If you ask someone to define the term 'spiral staircase', for example, he or she may well start off by talking of something that goes upwards and round and round, but then will almost instantaneously begin to twist his or her finger round and round in mid-air in an upwards direction. Such gesticulation is more valuable than speech in that particular situation and certainly helps out someone who is trying to define the concept. Someone faced with the problem of explaining 'zigzag' is also likely to turn to gesticulation fairly quickly.

Gesticulation is frequently used as a backup to speech when geometrical shapes are being described, as, for example, when someone is asked to describe a triangle or oblong without being too technical. It is also used in many other instances where the person speaking thinks that the words used are less than adequate to convey the desired meaning. Of course, it is often an involuntary backup rather than a planned one, the word flow of the definer suddenly having proved inadequate.

Directions

A classic example of this is the person who is asked by a motorist for directions to somewhere. The per-

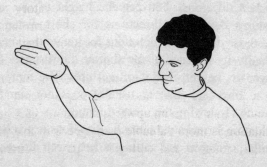

son giving the directions will not only embark on these verbally by saying something like, 'You go straight ahead at the next set of lights, turn right at the roundabout, then left at the church and go straight on until you come to a pub called the Red Lion, and it's the second on the right after that – you can't miss it,' but will be accompanying the spoken instructions by arm and hand gestures to illustrate the various turns the car should make. In this case the gesticulation is often more helpful to the person giving the instructions, since the arm actions seem to serve as a reminder to him or her of where the place in question is, than to the person at the receiving end of the instructions, who is sitting in the driving seat desperately trying either to memorise the directions or write them, and to whom the arm-waving may well not be visible anyhow. There is often a marked difference between the height of the arm gestures describing directions for short distances and those describing directions for longer distances. Usually it is a case of the shorter the distance the lower the height of the arm gestures. The motorist on a long-haul journey usually does not stand a chance of viewing the visual directions.

A more formal style of traffic directions is given by traffic policemen and traffic wardens. Such directions are mostly silent, unless the policeman or traffic warden has given way to temptation and is swearing in frustration, and are thus dealt with under voluntary gesture in the next chapter.

Involuntary gesticulation

Our need to enhance our speech with gesture is so great, and often so involuntary, that many of us frequently resort to gesticulation even when we are taking part in a telephone conversation and the other person has no opportunity to witness or interpret any gesticulation. For example, we may be complaining angrily to a representative of a firm who has not delivered something that we have ordered at the time promised. 'I want it delivered right here, right now!' we may shout, pointing with enraged emphasis at the floor to show exactly where 'here' is. Although this gesticulatory emphasis goes unseen by the person at the other end of the line, the shouting will usually have been enough to convey

the general tenor of how we are feeling. There is a therapeutic quality about this kind of gesticulation. It may not have had an effect on our telephone partner, but it has helped us to give vent to our anger and release the tension.

There are many gestures that can be used with or without speech and can thus be categorised both as examples of gesticulation and as examples of voluntary gesture – indeed, some can also appear in the third category of involuntary gesture.

Many of the gestures that can function either as gesticulation or as voluntary gesture are dealt with in the next chapter on voluntary gestures. This is particularly true of those gestures that are more commonly encountered without speech.

Examples of gesticulation

Gestures capable of being classified as examples of gesticulation but dealt with in the next chapter include the following, listed here from top to toe:

head
head-shaking	indicating agreement or acceptance
head-nodding	indicating refusal, denial or negation
head-patting	indicating self-congratulation

head-scratching   indicating puzzlement or bewilderment

head-slapping   indicating annoyance at the realisation that one has forgotten something or has suddenly remembered something too late

head-tossing   indicating defiance or aggressiveness or indicating a beckoning movement or indicating a sexual come-on

head-tilting   an indicatory movement, used instead of pointing or indicating a beckoning movement

brow
wiping with hand   indicating great heat or indicating a narrow escape

eyes
hands over eyes   indicating a desire not to see someone or something

eyebrows
eyebrow-raising   indicating shock, surprise or disapproval

Body Language

eyebrow-lowering
            indicating annoyance or concentration

ears

ear-cupping — indicating inability to hear or difficulty in hearing

fingers over ears — indicating a desire not to hear something or to express displeasure at noise

hands over ears — indicating a desire not to hear someone or something

nose

nose-tapping — indicating secrecy or confidentiality

nose-holding — indicating the presence of an unpleasant smell

nose-wrinkling — indicating disapproval or indicating the presence of an unpleasant smell

exaggerated sniff — indicating the presence of something with a pleasant smell, especially something good to eat

lips

lip-licking   indicating appreciative anticipation of something pleasant, especially something good to eat

finger on lips see finger

fingertip kissing see finger

kiss-blowing   indicating appreciation of something pleasant or indicating a farewell gesture

chin

chin-cupping   indicating deep thought

shoulders

shoulder-shrug   indicating ignorance or indifference

arms

arms akimbo   indicating anger

folded arms   indicating anger

arm-waving   indicating warning or 'keep off' gesture, indicating the presence of someone or something or indicating a greeting

Body Language

hands

hand-waving	indicating a gesture of farewell or indicating one's presence to attract attention
hand-clapping	indicating a conventional form of approval or appreciation
hand-raising	indicating one's presence to attract attention
hand-rubbing	indicating extreme cold or indicating pleasure or anticipation
hand-shaking	as a conventional form of greeting
hand-sweeping	indicating either 'after you' or indicating a 'go-away' gesture

hands over ears see ears

hands over eyes see eyes

fists

fist-raising	indicating aggression or intimidation

fingers

finger-raising	indicating one's presence to attract attention

| *finger at lips* | indicating a need for quiet or silence |

thumbs

| *raised thumb* | indicating approval or acceptance or indicating that everything is fine |

CHAPTER 2

Voluntary Gestures

Intentional emphasis

This chapter describes voluntary gestures, those body actions or gestures that are carried out quite intentionally, with the full awareness of the user of the gesture, unlike Chapter 3, Involuntary Gestures. Voluntary gestures, in terms of this book, are unaccompanied by speech. In this latter respect they are distinguished from Chapter 1, Gesticulations.

There is some overlap between the categories gesticulation and voluntary gestures since some gestures are capable of being used with or without speech. The presence or absence of speech will determine to which category they should be assigned.

Some of the gestures that have been described under gesticulations can also be used without speech and as such can also be described as voluntary gestures. An example of such a gesture is that of crossed fingers, which can be used without speech to indicate that the owner of the crossed fingers is hoping for good luck (*see* page 27).

Another example is that of the self-hug. This can be used to indicate extreme cold without accompanying speech. Sometimes there is a compromise between speech and non-speech when the person experiencing cold accompanies the self-hug with 'Brrrr!' (*see* page 24).

Also described under gesticulations but capable also of being used without speech is the gesture that indicates lack of knowledge of the whereabouts of someone or something. Throwing the arms wide from the body is enough to plead one's ignorance (*see* page 26).

Examples of gestures that can be used with or without speech but that have not been dealt with under gesticulations include wiping imaginary sweat from the brow (*see* page 25). If used alone it is capable of being misconstrued unless the meaning is absolutely clear from the context, as such a gesture can be associated either with extreme heat or with a narrow escape. The use of speech helps to clarify things. Where heat is involved, the wiper of the brow will exclaim something like, 'Gosh, it's hot!' or 'What a scorcher!' to accompany his or her action while, if some form of danger has just been averted, the accompanying statement will be of the order of 'Phew! That was a close thing!' or 'Gosh, they nearly caught us!'

Rubbing the hands

Rubbing of the hands is another gesture that can either be accompanied by speech or not. Again, in the absence of speech the gesture could be open to misinterpretation unless the meaning was crystal clear from the context. The gesture can mean that it is very cold, in which case it might be the accompaniment of 'Gosh, it's cold out here!' The same gesture can be used by someone who is commenting with pleasure or approval on something. In this case the gesture is often accompanied by a verbal comment, such as, 'Isn't this nice?'

Rubbing the hands can also be a sign that the person executing the gesture is anticipating something that he or she will find pleasure in. It is frequently a gesture that other people might find unpleasant, as when a miser is rubbing his hands at the thought of counting his money.

'After you'

Another example of a gesture that can be used with speech or not could occur if someone was being polite and was allowing someone else to precede him into a room. The person could either make a slow forward sweeping and graceful movement with his hand and say 'After you!' or he could make the gesture without saying anything at all. In this case the gesture is unlikely to be misinterpreted because it is clear from the context.

Pointing

The use of pointing, as with the index finger, for emphasis is also capable of being used either with or without speech. If it is used with speech then it simply backs up or emphasises the statement that is being made, as 'The book is on the table over there,' or 'I put the parcel over there by the door.' When used without speech it is frequently not used simply for emphasis but to demonstrate the direction in which someone should look in order to see or find the object, person or place. Pointing is most often accompanied by speech and is thus covered more fully in the previous chapter, Gesticulation.

Kissing the fingertips

The fingers are used in conjunction with the lips to form a gesture of extreme approval or appreciation. The gesture of kissing the fingertips rather lingeringly, which is Gallic in origin, tends to be used only by people given to rather dramatic theatrical gestures. It can be used as a voluntary gesture without speech. For example, someone might taste a particularly delicious piece of cake and kiss the fingertips in mock ecstasy. It can also be used with speech as a form of gesticulation (*see* other finger gestures, page 35), as when someone sips from a glass of exceptionally fine wine, kisses the fingertips and exclaims something along the lines of 'wonderful!' Those continuing with the Gallic theme may even exclaim, '*Magnifique!*'

People who indulge in kissing of the fingertips tend to do so to express their appreciation of something that they are eating or drinking. It is sometimes, however, used, mostly by men, to express appreciation of the beauty of a member of the opposite sex.

The kissing of the fingertips to express pleasure should not be confused with the kissing of the fingertips when blowing a kiss. In this case the kiss tends to be less lingering and is used as a gesture of farewell. It is usually used by women or from a man to a woman. This gesture can be used in conjunction with speech, such as 'Bye for now!' or 'See you soon!' and so becomes an example of gesticulation, but it is very frequently used across a room to someone not within earshot.

Licking the lips

The lips are involved in conjunction with the tongue to indicate anticipation of something good to eat. The gesture of licking the lips can be used either on its own or to accompany a remark such as 'That looks delicious!' Like rubbing the hands, it can be interpreted by others as rather an unpleasant gesture. This is particularly true when the gesture is used by someone, usually a man, salivating over the attractiveness of a member of the opposite sex, often accompanying the gesture by a demeaning remark, such as 'That looks tasty!'

Foot stamping

Some foot gestures can also be used accompanied or unaccompanied by speech. The stamping foot, described in the previous chapter on gesticulation (*see* page 35), is most usually accompanied by shouting or screaming as part of a tantrum, but it can occur on its own to indicate silent frustration.

Kicking

A forward kick with one foot is often used to indicate angrily that someone should get out or leave the presence of the person making the gesture. It can either be used without the benefit of speech or be accompanied by an exclamation, such as 'Get out!' or something more colourful. The gesture is often used to domestic pets – usually those belonging to someone else – whose presence is not welcome. In this case the forward kick is usually accompanied by 'Shoo!'

Forward sweep of the hand

A similar message can be assumed if someone sweeps the hand away from the body. Again it can be accompanied or unaccompanied by speech, although the former in this case is the more common. For example, a woman might say to someone trying to sell her something at the door, 'Get away with you,' and make a forward sweeping movement with her hand.

The nose-tap

The nose-tap is a common gesture in body language. This is often an involuntary gesture and has been treated as such in the next chapter (*see* page 153).

However, it can also be used as a voluntary gesture and even as gesticulation. In both of these contexts it is an indication of confidentiality or something secret or underhand. Someone gossiping over the fence to a neighbour might impart a piece of juicy scandal about another neighbour, saying 'Keep this to yourself but ...' or words to this effect, and tap his or her nose with the index finger. Alternatively, someone wishing to make a plea for secrecy, or wishing to indicate that something secret or underhand is going on in a situation where for some reason speech is not possible, may well make the same gesture.

Holding the nose
The nose is of course associated with smell. Holding

the nose by pinching the nostrils tightly together, often in rather a dramatic or theatrical way, is a voluntary gesture indicating that there is a bad or foul smell around, as when a companion has stepped in dog dirt. It is often used also as an example of gesticulation, since people often accompany the gesture by saying something along the lines of 'What a smell!' Occasionally the speech is restricted to an exclamation such as 'Phew!' as when someone smells a particularly strong-smelling cheese.

Wrinkling the nose

Nose-wrinkling is used as a less dramatic way of indicating that there is something, or someone, ill-smelling around. Again it can be used either accompanied or unaccompanied by speech. Unlike nose-holding, nose-wrinkling can indicate displeasure not associated with smell. For example, you might indi-

cate your displeasure at someone's bad behaviour in public by nose-wrinkling or indicate your disinclination to do something. Wrinkling the nose where smell is not involved can be accompanied by speech, as when you say, 'I don't really fancy that film,' and wrinkle your nose. It can also be used without speech, unconsciously as well as consciously. Thus, someone might offer you a selection of magazines, none of which appealed to you. You might say politely, 'How kind of you! I shall enjoy reading these,' but your nose could be wrinkling at the same time. This kind of subconscious gesture is discussed in the next chapter on involuntary gestures (*see* page 152).

Sniffing

The exaggerated, lengthy sniff usually indicates that the person doing the sniffing is expressing appreciation of a pleasant smell. The pleasant smell may emanate from someone using an expensive French perfume or from a vase of sweet-smelling roses, but it is usually associated with food. The lengthy sniff can be used as a voluntary gesture on its own, or it can be accompanied by an appreciative remark, such as 'Ah, something smells good!'

Chin-stroking

Chin-stroking is more commonly used as an involuntary gesture and it is treated under the chapter so entitled (*see* page 161). However, it is sometimes used as a voluntary gesture and sometimes as a form of gesticulation. In both of these cases, the stroking of the chin signals deep thought or contemplation. It is often used deliberately and theatrically to achieve

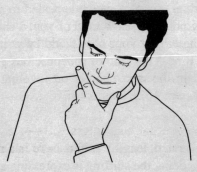

a humorous effect. For example, a father might indulge in the gesture when answering, 'Well, I don't know. I wonder if that could be arranged,' to a request made by his children for some kind of minor treat.

Ear-touching

Ear-touching is also common in body language. Again this is often an involuntary gesture, and as such has been dealt with in the next chapter (*see* page 149). One gesture involving the ear is, however, used as a voluntary gesture. If you wish to indicate to someone that you cannot hear what he or she is saying, for example, because of the level of noise around you, you would be likely to cup your hand around your ear to indicate this fact. It would be a fairly useless exercise if the noise level around you is excessive, but you could turn the ear-cupping into gesticulation by shouting, 'I can't hear you!'

It is quite obvious why the silent form of ear-cupping would be the most likely. Indeed, there are often several reasons why someone might choose to use the speechless form of a gesture. One reason is obviously when there is a need for silence.

The speechless gesture

'Hush!'

If a rowdy party of people is just about to enter a house where there is a fractious baby that has just got off to sleep there is very little point in the mother of the baby shouting, 'Be quiet! The baby is sleeping!' since the noise will wake the baby. The mother would be better to resort to the voluntary gesture and put a finger to her lips as a request for silence. As an alternative she could put her head to one side on folded hands to mimic someone sleeping and make a plea for silence in this way – although this mime can also indicate that the person performing it is tired and wants to go sleep. The mother requesting silence could, of course, accompany her mime with a 'Hush!' or with a whispered 'You'll wake the baby!' in which case her voluntary gesture would become a gesticulation according to the system of categorisation in this book.

The speechless gesture is extremely useful when something has to be communicated silently or discreetly so that someone will remain unaware of it. If you know that a friend is just about to say something less than flattering about someone who is in within earshot, you can prevent a sticky situation by using some form of mime to indicate to your friend the presence of the person concerned. You might nod or tilt your head in the direction of the person to bring your friend's attention to him or her or you might discreetly use your thumb to the same effect.

Of course, it need not be a person whose presence you are discreetly indicating. It might be something that you think will interest, shock or amuse your companion. For example, you might be in someone's house and wish to point out to a friend a particularly ugly piece of furniture or an ornament. Obviously, you cannot comment aloud or the owner of the house will hear you, and the pointing finger would be easily spotted. However, a nod or tilt of the head or a thrust of the thumb will indicate what you want to communicate without offence being caused.

Trouble

There are many occasions in which the speechless gesture will speak volumes without involving you in any unpleasantness. You might wish to indicate to a colleague at work that another colleague, who is within earshot but who is not actually looking at you at the time, is going to get into great trouble. Since you are unable to put this into words for fear of being overheard, you draw an imagi-

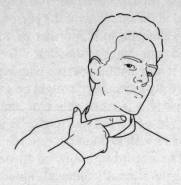

nary line with the edge of your hand across your throat as if you were drawing a sword across it, signifying death. In fact, the symbolic gesture sometimes signifies real death, rather than great trouble, since it can indicate that someone has committed suicide.

Where silence and secrecy are not issues to be considered, the above gesture can be used with speech and so becomes an example of gesticulation. In this case the gesture is used to add colourful emphasis to a rather gloomy statement, such as 'He's had it now!' 'The boss wants to see her – she's for the chop!' or 'If the headmaster finds out what they've been up to, they're for it!' There is often an element of somewhat ghoulish enjoy-

ment at the misfortune of others in this gesture. It would be unusual for the person making the gesture to be the person whose fate or life is at risk.

A voluntary gesture that also indicates either severe trouble, or suicide, death or trouble, is that of pointing the forefinger at the temple with the thumb in the air. The gesture is symbolic of pointing a pistol at the head.

Madness
The voluntary gesture without speech can be used to humorous effect. If you are standing behind someone who is busily haranguing a group of people, and you wish to indicate to the others that you think that he is either a fool or quite mad, you can describe a

circle in the air beside your temple or ear to indicate that his brains are scrambled and that he is a fool. Alternatively, you can tap the side of your forehead to indicate the same thing, the only problem being that this same gesture can also mean, especially in the United States, that the person in question is very bright, something of an egghead in fact.

The intentional yawn

Similarly, you can open your mouth wide and put your hand to it to simulate a yawn. This gesture is used to indicate to that you are bored. It is most often performed behind the bore's back to amuse any onlookers, but if the level of boredom is high enough and desperate measures are called for, then a more full-frontal method is required. This yawning gesture is frequently performed as an unconscious

ment of the result of some form of voting poll one of them might make the nail-biting gesture to his or her friend across the room.

Communicating over a distance

The voluntary gesture is much more useful either than speech alone or gesticulation where distance is a factor. The distance need not be very great – just enough to make ordinary communication difficult or impossible. People wishing to hitch a lift would obviously find it difficult to communicate with the drivers of passing vehicles by any other means and so they stretch out their arms and stick their thumbs in the air, sometimes moving them from side to side.

Traffic direction signals

One set of people who rely heavily on voluntary gestures at relatively short distances are traffic policemen or traffic wardens. Such people are not so common now, in these days of complex traffic lights and roundabouts, but they are still to be found, especially when the said complex traffic lights have broken down. There you will find them, in the middle of a busy road at the height of the rush hour, using their hands and arms to indicate to motorists whether to halt or proceed.

Body Language

Al an auction

People bidding at auctions are also regularly involved in voluntary gestures at reasonably short distances. The actual nature of the gesture varies from person to person. Such gestures include the raising of a hand, the raising of a finger, or the waving of a piece of paper, but can be less obvious, such as the

touching of an ear lobe or the rubbing of the nose. Those attending an auction but not intending to buy should be very careful that they do not make any gesture that could possibly be construed as a bid offer. Otherwise they might end up as the unwilling owners of something that they would not give house room to. Auctioneering is a skilled job, and some of this skill depends on the auctioneers interpreting the body language of the potential bidders sitting or standing in front of them. They become skilled not only in translating body actions as bid offers but also at assessing subconscious gestures and body posture to help them decide which members of the audience are the serious bidders and which are just there for interest or in the hope of picking up some low-cost trinket.

Tick-tack

When greater distances are involved, the voluntary gesture is even more useful. Those attending race-courses will be familiar with tick-tack, also spelt tic-tac, a system of manual semaphore signalling by which bookmakers make a series of arm-waving gestures to exchange information.

Pointing

Gestures that are able to be interpreted at long dis-tance are not, of course, restricted to the racecourse. They are of great use in everyday life. For example, you and some other people may be looking for something over quite a wide area and you happen to find it. You can, of course, try shouting to attract the attention of the others, but your words may well get lost in the wind. Provided the other members of the group are in possession of reasonable eyesight, it would almost certainly be more effective simply to raise your arm high with hand outstretched and point to the part of the ground where you have located what is being looked for.

Waving or drowning? – misinterpretation

The use of the voluntary gesture to overcome the problems of distance is very common. For example, someone who is in the middle of a crowd and has just spotted a friend in the distance may well raise a hand in the air and wave frantically to attract the friend's attention, since shouting either would not be heard or might cause embarrassment to the ultrashy.

Speech does have one great advantage over the speechless gesture. It is less likely to be misinterpreted. If you are at a distance from a group of people and are trying to warn them not to come any nearer because there is some form of danger, it is sometimes difficult to convey this fact. Because of distance, speech is impossible, but will they understand the gesture?

Warnings

For example, you are out walking on the hills with a

group of friends and you suddenly find yourself
some distance ahead of them and in decidedly
boggy terrain. Having almost got sucked into it
yourself, you are anxious to spare them this fate and
make attempts to stop them from following you, as
they have started to do. Your best bet is probably to
wave your arms frantically above your head, crossing and uncrossing them as you do so, to indicate
that you are in a no-go area and that they should not
proceed, but they may misinterpret the gesture and
think you are simply waving to attract their attention
and indicate your presence.

It would be too bad if they interpreted your arm-waving as being an indication of great joy or celebration and

rushed towards you to investigate the reason for this. We are used to seeing this kind of arm-waving on football fields, when players rush around waving their arms in glee, usually before hugging and kissing each other.

In your attempt to prevent your friends from following in your footsteps to soggy ground, it would be possible for you to raise your arms above your head with outstretched palms and move them backwards and forwards to indicate that they should not proceed, but again the effect of this would be by no means certain. At a distance the significance of this gesture could be lost. For the same reason, shaking the head from side to side to indicate something negative might scarcely be any more effective than speech.

Waving one hand would be considerably less effective than waving both arms about. In any case, waving the hand can be a problematic gesture generally, since it is used for more than one situation. If you wave the hand from side to side, you can be doing so to indicate that you are saying goodbye to someone (although some people, particularly children, wave the fingers of their hands up and down to do this), but you can use the same gesture either to indicate your presence and to attract someone's attention, or you can use it to say 'no'. One can only hope that the meaning

will be obvious from the context. In the particular
one under discussion, your friends might well assume
that you were either indicating your presence or in-
viting them to join you.

Shrugging
Sometimes a gesture that is open to misinterpretation can be helped if the user of the gesture is close
enough at hand for the expression on his or her face
to be seen.

A prolonged deep shrug of the shoulders is an indication that the person doing the shrugging does not know
the answer to something. The shrug, however, can also
indicate that he or she not only does not know but
does not care. Whether or not the gesture is meant to
convey both attitudes will be obvious from the person's expression.

Bridging the language gap
Gestures are perhaps sometimes more open to misinterpretation than speech, but they are a more in-
stant, more economic and often more expressive
way of getting one's message across. They are particularly useful when two people who do not know
each other's languages are trying to communicate. It
is pointless simply trying to shout at the other per-

son. If he does not understand when you are speaking in a normal tone of voice there is absolutely no reason why increasing the volume of your voice should increase his level of understanding. It is much better to try gestures or mime. In fact, an extension of this is found in the use of Sign Language by people who are deaf.

If you require access to a telephone and are in a restaurant or bar where neither the owner nor anyone else understands your language, you can try holding an imaginary telephone to your ear. The other people in the place will either direct you to the nearest telephone or assume that you are mad. Similarly, if you wish to ask someone without access to a common language if he or she would like a drink you could try pointing to the bottle, pointing at him or her and then raising an imaginary glass to your lips. The reaction might depend on your success as a mime artist or perhaps on how thirsty he or she is.

Gestures without speech, then, can be very useful in negotiating communication barriers caused by language barriers, but they can create problems when people of different cultures are trying to communicate. The problem is that the same sign can mean different things to different people.

Cultural differences and misunderstandings
V for victory
One obvious example is the sign signifying victory, popularised by Winston Churchill, the British war leader. Called the V-sign, it is made by the index and

middle finger of the hand in the shape of the letter V. This is a common sign internationally, sometimes being used to designate peace as well as victory.

*V for ** *****!*
In Britain, however, unlike in some other countries, the position of the palm of the hand is all-important. If the palm is turned outwards, facing away from the person making the gesture, then that denotes victory, but if the palm is turned inwards facing the person

who is making the gesture, then the sign is considered to be very offensive and has nothing to do with victory, and certainly not with peace.

Indeed, it is an insulting and aggressive sign, made even more so if the gesture is executed with a swift upward jerk of the fingers held aloft. It would translate into speech as 'Up yours!' and is considered just as offensive as the remark. Such a gesture is frequently seen on motorways as motorists indicate their displeasure at other motorists who have inconvenienced them in some way. Visitors from other countries who use what they think is the victory sign without appreciating the problem of the position of the palm may live to regret it dearly. Imagine a supporter of a foreign football team indicating his delight at his team's success by using the V-sign and getting it wrong.

Signs using the thumb

Gestures indicating agreement or satisfaction can cause as many problems as the sign for victory. The use of a raised thumb to indicate approval or acceptance, or to indicate that everything is all right, is widely used internationally – just as is the thumb turned to point downwards to indicate disapproval, refusal or to indicate that everything is far from all right.

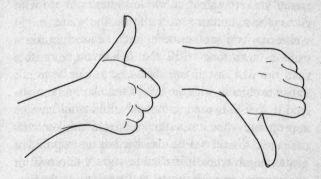

However, the raised thumb can get you into trouble in some parts of the world. Its use is best avoided in Australia because if you should jerk the raised thumb upwards, even by accident, it will be construed as an offensive gesture meaning the same to an Australian as the V-sign with the palm turned inwards to the British, in other words a more visual way of communicating 'Up yours!' It might have unfortunate consequences if you were indicating to a friend across an Australian room that you were fine and someone jogged your arm.

The raised thumb, even when used by hitchhikers, can also be taken as a very rude gesture in some countries, particularly Nigeria. It causes problems of a less serious kind in Germany. There, if you raised your thumb in a bar to indicate to a friend across the room that you were fine, the waiter might well bring you another beer, since a raised thumb is used to mean 'one'. Still, that is a much better fate than you will sustain in either Australia or Nigeria.

The problems with the raised thumb can be obviated if speech is used. Obviously, this would not be appropriate when it is a sign used by hitchhikers, but the raised thumb can be classified as an example of gesticulation when it is used to signify approval or acceptance, or to indicate that everything is fine. Thus, someone wishing to indicate that some kind of proceedings can begin might raise a thumb and say something along the lines of 'All systems go!'

Thumb and forefinger forming a circle

But we are not yet finished with problems associated with gestures that indicate that everything is OK. The Americans, in particular, can get into trouble, as can anyone else who copies their habit of indicating that everything is fine or agreed by forming a circle with thumb and forefinger and splaying the other three fingers upwards. The gesture indicates precision, or possibly represents the 'O' of 'OK',

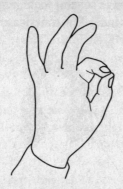

but in many parts of the world this sign is taken to represent the anus or the vagina and to be extremely offensive, suggesting either 'Up yours!' or that the person to whom the gesture is directed is an 'asshole'. In France, the same sign means 'nothing' or

'worthless' and can be taken as an insult but not to
the same extent.

The raised hand

One of the most common gestures of all can cause
so much confusion, whether at home or abroad, that
it is enough to make us all start reverting to speech
immediately. The gesture is that of the raised hand.
Depending on the intention of the person making the
gesture this can have several meanings. It can mean
'hello!' or 'hi!' – indeed in American Western films

the American Indians are often depicted as raising a
hand and saying 'How!' when they are greeting the
white men, a gesture much copied by children when

they are playing Cowboys and Indians. It can also mean the opposite – 'goodbye' – particularly when the person making the gesture is rather laid-back, the raised hand taking less effort than the enthusiastically waved hand.

The raised hand, like the wave, can also be used to indicate a person's whereabouts, the nonverbal equivalent of 'Here I am!' or 'Over here!' Perhaps as a kind of extended version of this, it can also be used to beckon someone, particularly a waiter in a restaurant or bar. In this respect it carries overtones of the classroom, where it is used to attract the attention of the teacher.

Some confusion can also arise with the raised finger. It can, like the raised hand and the wave, be used as an indication of a person's whereabouts, and it can also be used to beckon to a waiter. In addition,

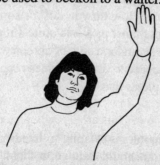

it can mean that the person making the gesture wants one, as opposed to two or three, of something. To some extent it depends on how you raise your finger. If you raise it very straight and stiffly with the rest of the fingers curled up in the palm and facing away from you, it indicates a very offensive insult, meaning the same as the reverse V-sign – 'up yours!' The gesture is made even more offensive if the finger is jerked upwards.

The handshake

The handshake is one of the voluntary gestures that you would think least likely to cause confusion or misinterpretation.

The handshake need not, of course, be a silent gesture. It is frequently used with speech, as when two people being introduced for the first time shake hands and say, 'How do you do!' or something less formal. For the most part it is quite simply a standard sign of greeting or a sign of agreement, as on the signing of a peace treaty or business contract. But it is not as simple as that.

Frequency

One of the problems relating to handshakes is how frequently you should indulge in them. This varies quite significantly from country to country. The French seem addicted to the habit when they are not exchanging kisses on the cheek. The British are considerably more restrained.

Type
Then there is the question of the type of handshake. The Scandinavians indulge in a single press of the hand of short duration, people from the Middle Eastern countries tend to go in for handshakes with a gentle grip, while Americans and some British men think it appropriate to give a good firm grip that will have the recipient wincing with pain in order to stress their sincerity, honesty, and general strength of character and virility. This concern with openness may have associations with the origins of the handshake, the outstretched hand having originally been taken as a sign that the owner of the hand was not in possession of a weapon. Many people overdo the power of their handshakes, sometimes to try to disguise the fact that they are not in fact open and honest but are lying or are being economical with the truth.

The limp handshake
The limp handshake is often wrongly taken to be a

sure sign of a wimp. This is by no means always the case. As has been pointed out above, this can be a matter of culture and geography since people from some countries, such as those located in the Middle East, tend by custom to go for a gentle handshake, irrespective of the degree of their honesty, sincerity or strength of character. Others, too, can be perfectly sincere and strong in character, but they have some reason for avoiding the knuckle-bruising handshake. Such people include anyone who is suffering from any medical complaint involving pain or discomfort to the hands, such as arthritis, or anyone who by profession or position has to shake hands exceptionally frequently, such as a member of royalty or a senior politician. Self-preservation, or rather finger-preservation, dictates that they keep their hands as limp and as passive as possible.

To kiss or not?
There are other problems associated with handshakes, principally the fact that in not every country is the handshake used as a greeting. People from southern Europe and Latin American frequently kiss each other on the cheek or embrace, the Japanese bow, and the Maoris from New Zealand rub noses. Saying hello can be complicated.

The fist
The fist as well as the hand is likely to be involved in a degree of misinterpretation. It is widely held to be a symbol of aggression, being used by opponents to hit each other in a boxing match or other less formal form of fight, and is often used as such.

Anger
For example, a farmer might shake his fist at children who have stolen apples from his orchard and are in the process of running away. Likewise, a motorist who has had his car damaged by a car whose driver has just driven away might indulge in the same aggressive gesture, although he would do better to take the number of the culprit's car.

When the raised fist is a sign of aggression it is sometimes accompanied by speech, although being rather a graphic gesture it does not really require the benefit of speech. However, someone may well raise the fist in a threatening gesture and say something like, 'If you don't get out of here, you'll be for it.'

Power, victory or pride
The raised closed fist is not always a symbol of aggression. It all depends on the direction in which the fist is facing. If the closed fingers are facing the per-

son who is making the gesture then aggression can be assumed. If they are facing away from the person then the fist is likely to be a symbol of power, victory or pride.

The upraised fist with the fingers turned outwards became synonymous with the 'Black Power' movement in the United States of America. Since then it has come to be used regularly by people congratulating themselves on something. Someone leaving an interview, having heard that he or she had just got a job, might well use such a gesture in silent triumph. Indeed, punching in the air conveys much the same sentiments as the high-five salute, where two people slap palms in the air in celebration or victory. If there is only one person doing the celebrating, a high slapping movement with the palm of the hand in the air is sometimes executed.

Hand clapping

Another gesture involving the hands that is mostly straightforward in its interpretation but is capable of some confusion is that of hand-clapping. It is the classic conventional form of applause by which an audience shows its appreciation and approval of a performance. The fervour with which people carry out the gesture varies according to the genuineness of their enthusiasm. The hand-clapping that follows a run-of-the-mill speech at the Annual General

Meeting of a firm or association is likely to be weak and low-key, with rather limp hands scarcely meeting each other. On the other hand, the applause at a concert that the audience has enjoyed very much is likely to consist of strong, enthusiastic hand-slapping. It may even lead to a standing ovation, when the audience stands and applauds wildly.

The element of slight confusion comes in when the hand-clapping is slow and rhythmical. This can just be a sign that the audience has been indulging in a spell of passionate hand-slapping for a considerable time and has reduced the strength and speed of the hand-clapping for the sake of their hands.

However, slow hand-clapping can be a sign of impatience on the part of the audience if the person whom they are there to hear or see fails to turn up on time. It can also be a sign that they are bored, as a comedian who is failing to hold the audience's interest may well find out.

In some countries, such as some European countries, the slow rhythmical handclap may not be a sign of impatience or boredom on the part of the audience. The audience may just be applauding in time to the rhythm of the music, particularly if the entertainment being provided is ice-skating or ice-dancing.

For the most part, hand-clapping is self-explanatory and has no need of speech. If speech is present it usually takes the form of 'Bravo!' 'Encore!' or 'More!'

Nodding and shaking the head

Nodding and shaking of the head are among the most common gestures in body language, and one would be forgiven if one thought that they would be self-evident, that nodding would always be a positive sign, a sign of agreement, and that shaking of the head would always be a negative sign, a sign of disagreement. Indeed, the gestures are thought to mimic a baby respectively accepting the mother's breast and rejecting it.

In Britain, head-nodding and head-shaking generally live up to one's expectations about them as markers, respectively, of agreement and acceptance or of negation and denial. Both head-nodding and head-shaking being used both intentionally and subconsciously can be ranked both as voluntary and involuntary gestures. As involuntary gestures they are dealt with in the next chapter. Both nodding of the head and shaking of the head can be used as an accompaniment to speech and consequently can also be ranked as a form of gesticulation. In this respect they are used for emphasis. Thus we might encounter someone nodding the head vigorously in eager acceptance of an offer, saying, 'Yes, I'd love to go!' or someone else shaking the head and denying all knowledge of something or someone, saying 'No, I've never heard of them.'

A single nod
A single nod of the head is a sign of greeting or acknowledgement, of the kind given by neighbours to each other when they pass in the street. A more formal version of this is a bow, a fuller form of the nod.

Cultural differences
All is, however, not plain sailing with head-nodding and head-shaking. Problems occur with these gestures when other countries and other cultures are involved. In some countries, such as Bulgaria and parts of Greece and Turkey, nodding the head can mean 'no' and shaking the head can mean 'yes'. You can well imagine the degree of confusion that this could cause.

Tossing the head
Tossing the head can also cause confusion. In Britain it is often a sign of defiance or aggrievedness

and is capable of being ranked as gesticulation, voluntary gesture or involuntary gesture (*see* page 127), according to whether it is accompanied by speech, used silently but consciously, or used subconsciously. A typical example of it being used intentionally as a gesture of defiance would be a teenage girl storming out of the house after being told by her mother to stay put and do her homework, tossing her head the while. If accompanied by speech the comment would be along the lines of, 'I'll do what I like, and you can't stop me!'

Head-tossing, however, does not always signify that someone is being defiant or aggrieved. It can also be used voluntarily or involuntarily in Britain as a sexual come-on or simply as an indication of vanity.

Some gestures are more often used by members of one sex than the other. Both as a sign of defiance or as a sexual come-on, the tossing head is a gesture most commonly used by women or girls, the gesture being particularly effective when the woman or girl concerned has long hair. The gesture is, however, sometimes used by homosexual men, often in a deliberately exaggerated or camped-up way. Because of this, it is used by others to caricature gay men.

Tossing the head has yet another common use that

is totally unisexual, in that it is used equally commonly by men and women. Like tilting or jerking the head, it can be used as a beckoning motion or as a signal to indicate something or someone. Thus, if you wish to indicate to a friend at a party that someone whom he or she dislikes strongly and so will want to avoid has just entered the room, you may well toss your head in the direction of the person who has just come in so that your friend will look over and take appropriate action. Alternatively, if you wish to indicate to a friend that he or she should join you, you could toss your head. If, however, the person so summoned is not a friend but a relative stranger or a waiter, the gesture is considered rude.

From all this it will be obvious that head-tossing can cause a few problems, and confusion is further heightened when different cultures are involved. In Greece, Malta and some other countries, a toss of the head can mean 'no'. Perhaps it is an aspect of body language best avoided unless the meaning is crystal clear from the context or unless it has the benefit of backup speech.

Obvious gestures
Thumbing the nose
With all this room for uncertainty, it is a positive re-

lief to come across a gesture that is confusion-free. The sign known as thumbing the nose is difficult to misconstrue since it is a clear, obvious insult. A gesture beloved by children, it is made by placing the thumb of one hand on the tip of the nose with the other fingers splayed outward, and often making a wiggling movement. Since the gesture clearly speaks for itself, it is hardly ever accompanied by speech, although 'Sucks to you!' is a possible accompaniment.

Another gesture much liked by children is the sticking out of one's tongue. When this is a voluntary gesture it is rude and insulting, in much the same way as thumbing one's nose is, and again does not need the benefit of speech. However, the stick-

ing out of one's tongue is not necessarily an indication of insult. Some people stick out their tongues
quite involuntarily when they are concentrating
hard, and so the gesture can be an example of an involuntary gesture, of the kind treated in the next section of the book (*see* page 158). The two situations
are not likely to be confused since it is usually
abundantly clear when someone is insulting you
and usually equally clear when someone is concentrating.

Either voluntary or involuntary gestures
Unfortunately, not all examples of voluntary ges-

tures are as clear-cut as thumbing the nose and sticking out the tongue. Voluntary gestures can be a dangerous minefield for the unwary, and one or two unfortunate experiences could leave you thinking that you had better stick to speech and keep your hands and arms out of harm's way. It is not easy to do this, and it is even more difficult in the case of involuntary gestures, subject of the next chapter.

We have seen how there is great deal of overlap between gesticulation and involuntary gesture. To add to the confusion that besets body language, some gestures can be either voluntary gestures or involuntary gestures, depending on whether the user is deliberately performing the gesture to create an intended effect or whether it is a completely unconscious gesture, executed almost as a habit.

Arms akimbo – anger

The gesture involving arms akimbo is a case in point. This gesture is achieved by putting one's arms at one's sides with one's elbows raised to form a kind of triangular shape. A person might stand deliberately with arms akimbo to emphasise the degree of anger or outrage felt, as in the case of a mother confronting a teenage son or daughter who has returned home after the agreed or promised time. This would obviously be an example of a voluntary gesture, and indeed is capable of being turned into an example of gesticulation by the addition of an appropriate remark, such as 'And where might you have been?' On the other hand, someone might adopt a similar gesture unconsciously, also in response to feelings of anger.

Whether the gesture is intentional or not, only the user of the gesture knows, but in either event the message conveyed is quite clear to the receiver of the gesture. It is time to apologise profusely or beat a hasty retreat – probably both.

In domestic comedies on stage and screen the arms akimbo gesture is the hallmark of the outraged, angry wife. Someone using the gesture offstage might do so to create a humorous or satirical effect. Thus, he or she might not be really angry but putting on an act to simulate anger, true feelings being conveyed by facial expression.

Anger might be expressed with only one arm adopting the arms akimbo stance. This gesture can be an intentional expression of one's annoyance or displeasure, but it can also be used unconsciously by someone expressing the same feelings and so is also an example of an involuntary gesture and dealt with in the following chapter (*see* page 167).

It should be remembered, however, that the single arm at the side with the elbow raised can, in fact, be a version of the hand on hip with raised elbow. Both these gestures are frequently used by models on the catwalk as they are showing off fashion clothes, and such cases are obviously voluntary gestures. The two allied gestures can also be performed by women to attract members of the opposite sex. In this respect the gestures are intentional, but they are often unconscious and so are examples of involuntary gestures and, as such, are dealt with in the next chapter (*see* page 168).

Tapping the foot

Tapping the foot can also be used either consciously or unconsciously. The gesture is frequently used quite intentionally, most usually by women, to emphasise their impatience or annoyance and to make their feelings abundantly clear to others. A woman waiting outside a cinema for an unpunctual escort may well be tapping the pavement with the toe of her shoe with great vigour, but only she will know whether the gesture is conscious or not. In either event, she may well accompany the gesture by frequent glances at her watch. The gesture is evocative enough not to require speech, although it may be accompanied by something along the lines of, 'Where on earth is he?' uttered through clenched teeth. Incidentally, clenched teeth are also common in body language, but, although the gesture can be used quite intentionally by someone wishing to express anger or intimidation, it is more usually an example of involuntary gesture and as such is dealt with in the next chapter (*see* page 197).

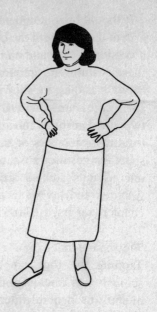

In common with the arms akimbo gesture, the tapping foot gesture can be executed for humorous or satirical effect to indicate that the person performing the gesture has a right to be annoyed or impatient, although he or she is not in fact so. The true situation can be deduced from facial expression or from context.

Arm folding

What has been said about the arms akimbo and foot-tapping gestures is also true of the arm-folding gesture when this is an indication of anger. The person performing the gesture may either be aware or unaware of the action and may even be doing so for fun. If the arm-folder is performing the gesture quite deliberately then speech might also be involved, as when an irate mother greets the late arrival of one of her children with folded arms and the icy comment, 'And what time do you call this?'

Arm-folding is not always a sign of anger. When it is not, it is usually an example of an involuntary gesture, suggesting a defensive or withdrawn attitude, and as such is dealt with in depth in the chapter on involuntary gestures (*see* page 168).

Scratching the head

Other gestures that can be used intentionally or otherwise and so can qualify either as voluntary gestures or involuntary gestures include scratching or slapping the head. The first of these indicates puzzlement, and the head-scratcher can be using it deliberately to emphasise lack of knowledge or bewilderment, sometimes in a theatrical, camped-up way, or can be using it quite unconsciously as a habit to which he or she automatically turns in moments of puzzlement or uncertainty. Especially when used for humorous effect, the act of head-scratching can also be accompanied by speech, becoming an instance of gesticulation. For example, a grandfather may say to his granddaughter, 'I did have a present for you. Now, where did I put it?' scratching his head in exaggerated bewilderment and looking around the place just to tease her.

Running fingers through hair

Running the fingers through the hair is another gesture that can be classified either as a voluntary gesture or an involuntary gesture. When performing it unconsciously, the maker of the gesture is wishing to express extreme frustration, anger or desperation so that the people around him or her, who have prob-

The putting of the hand over the eyes as a voluntary gesture does not always indicate that the person making the gesture wishes to blot out physically something that is happening. The gesture can also indicate frustration, annoyance or disappointment. When it carries this meaning, the gesture is sometimes turned into an example of gesticulation by the maker of the gesture saying something along the lines of, 'Oh no! Why did that have to happen now?'

It can also be classified as an involuntary gesture when it is a more sketchy, less definite gesture, and this is dealt with in the next chapter.

The gesture made by putting the hand over the eyes is one of those gestures that is capable of having several meanings. It can also be a sign of great tiredness. As such it is frequently an example of a voluntary gesture but a more less definite, sketchier form of it can be found as an example of an involuntary gesture. When the gesture is made by someone wearing spectacles, it is usual for the person to remove them, as though suffering from eye strain.

Fingers in the ears

Sometimes people find it necessary to shut out not the sight of something but the sound or noise of something. In such cases they can put their fingers in the ears, a gesture much used by children, when for once they themselves are not the cause of the noise. What they are trying to blot out can be either some piece of information they would rather not know about, or some form of noise that is either generally unpleasant or is interfering in some way with what they are doing.

The action is usually a voluntary gesture, but it is sometimes backed up by speech and so can be an example of gesticulation. For example, someone may say, 'What's that awful noise?' and stick his or her fingers in the ears. The gesture can be used in humorous contexts, as when someone puts the fingers in the ears when someone else is playing the violin in quite a musical way.

Hands over the ears

The desire to block out sound or noise can be indicated not only by putting the fingers in the ears but also by putting one's hands over one's ears. The gesture may not be physically so effective a method of shutting out noise, but it conveys the same message. Again, it is often an example of a voluntary gesture, but it is capable also of being used with speech and as such can be an example of gesticulation. For example, you might put your hands over your ears when shouting, 'For goodness' sake, turn that radio down!' In common with putting the fingers in the ears, the gesture can also be used in a humorous way.

As is the case with putting the hands over the eyes, so putting the hands over the ears can be an example of an involuntary gesture (*see* page 150). Again, as an involuntary gesture it is a more minimal, sketchier gesture. In such a situation the gesture can indicate much the same as the hand over the eyes, that the person performing the gesture is trying to shut out the whole of the set of circumstances surrounding him or her.

The wink

The wink is usually a voluntary gesture. The action can sometimes be an involuntary gesture (*see* page 148), but then it takes the from of a nervous tic.

Body Language

It might occasionally be accompanied by speech, but in fact it tends to rely for its effect on its secrecy or slyness and so is most usually silent. For example, one person might wink at a second person behind a third person's back in acknowledgement of the fact that the third person is in ignorance of something which the other two both know.

Winking need not necessarily indicate a shared secret. It can also be a sexual come-on or an attempt at silent chatting-up. Unlike tossing of the head as a sexual come-on, winking tends more to be the province of men than women. Although it is by no means unknown for  a woman to wink at a man for whom she has a fancy, it is nevertheless much more likely for a man to wink at the woman.

People who wink too lasciviously, or worse, make a lewd kissing noise with rounded lips, are in danger of being at the receiving end of a piece of body language over which there is very little doubt – the face-slap. If it is a resounding slap it has no need of words, but if words are provided they are usually short and to the point, usually 'Take that!'

So much for those gestures that we mean to make. Such gestures can reveal a great deal about our personalities to other people, but at least we have some control over them. It is often the gestures that we make unwittingly that give people a true insight into the real us, although we may not want them to. These gestures in this book are designated involuntary gestures and are dealt with in the next chapter.

A great many body language gestures have been described in this chapter. For ease of reference, listed below are the voluntary gestures mentioned above, arranged in top-to-toe order:

Examples of voluntary gestures

head

head-shaking	indicating agreement or acceptance
head-nodding	indicating refusal, denial or negation
head-bowing	indicating a formal greeting
head-patting	indicating self-congratulation
head-scratching	indicating puzzlement or confusion
head-slapping	indicating annoyance at the realisation that one has forgotten something or has suddenly remembered something too late

Body Language

head-tilting   an indicatory gesture used as a substitute for finger-pointing

head-tossing   indicating defiance or aggression or indicating a beckoning movement or indicating a sexual come-on

hair

running fingers through hair
      indicating frustration or anger

brow

furrowed brow   indicating worry or indicating anger

brow-wiping   indicating great heat or indicating a narrow escape

eyes

hands over eyes   indicating a desire not to see someone or something or indicating anger, frustration or disappointment

winking   indicating secrecy or slyness or indicating a sexual come-on.

edge of hand placed above eyes
      indicating difficulty seeing properly

eyebrows

single eyebrow raising
     indicating inquiry, surprise or
     disapproval

eyebrow-raising indicating surprise or disapproval

eyebrow-lowering indicating anger or disapproval

ears

ear-cupping indicating difficulty in hearing or
     an inability to hear properly

fingers in ears indicating a desire not to hear
     something

hands over ears indicating a desire not to hear
     something or indicating frustra-
     tion and annoyance

circle described in air round ear
     indicating stupidity

nose

nose-holding indicating the presence of an
     unpleasant smell

nose-tapping indicating confidentiality or secrecy

nose-wrinkling indicating the presence of an
     unpleasant smell or indicating
     distaste or disinclination

Body Language

exaggerated sniff indicating the presence of a pleasant smell, particularly the smell of food

thumb on nose indicating a gesture of rudeness

mouth
opening mouth wide in yawning
           indicating boredom or tiredness.

lips
lip-licking indicating anticipation of something pleasant, particularly something good to eat

fingers on lips indicating an informal gesture of greeting, as in blowing a kiss, or indicating approval or appreciation

tongue
tongue sticking far out
           indicating a gesture of rudeness

tongue sticking out partially
           indicating concentration

chin
chin-stroking indicating deep thought

throat

hand drawn across throat
> indicating trouble or death

shoulders

shrugging   indicating ignorance or indifference

arms

arm-folding   indicating anger or, in the form of a
self-hug, indicating extreme cold

arms resting on hips
> indicating anger

one arm resting on hip
> indicating vanity or a sexual come-on

arm-waving   indicating one's presence so as to
attract attention

arm-waving   indicating a warning 'keep-away'
gesture

arm-waving   indicating joy and celebration

arms out wide   indicating lack of knowledge

hand

hand-waving   indicating a conventional gesture
of farewell or indicating one's
presence to attract attention

hand-clapping	indicating a conventional form of approval or appreciation
hand-raising	indicating one's presence to attract attention
hand-rubbing	indicating extreme cold or indicating pleasure or anticipation
hand-shaking	indicating a conventional form of greeting
hand-sweeping	indicating an 'after-you' gesture or indicating a 'go-away' gesture
hands over ears	indicating a desire not to see someone or something or indicating frustration or anger
hands over eyes	indicating a desire not to see someone or something

fists

fist-raising (palm inwards)
  indicating aggression or intimidation

fist-raising (palm outwards)
  indicating power, victory or celebration

fingers

finger-raising   indicating one's presence so as to attract attention or indicating a request for one of something or indicating an offensive gesture

finger on closed lips
indicating a need for quiet or silence

fingers on pursed lips
indicating approval or appreciation

fingers on lips   indicating an informal gesture of farewell, as in kiss-blowing

fingers in V shape (palm outwards)
indicating victory or peace

fingers in V shape (palm inwards)
indicating an offensive gesture

crossed fingers   indicating a wish for good luck

thumbs

thumb on nose   indicating a gesture of rudeness

thumb-pointing   indicating an indicatory gesture as a substitute for finger-pointing

thumb-raising   as hitchhiking sign

Body Language

thumb and finger forming circle
> indicating that everything is OK

thumb-raising indicating acceptance, approval or that everything is all right or indicating that something can begin

thumb turned downwards
> indicating refusal or disapproval or that everything is not all right

feet

foot-tapping indicating anger or impatience

foot-stamping indicating anger

forward kick indicating a 'go-away' gesture

CHAPTER 3

Involuntary Gestures

Habit, convention and true self

It would be difficult to prevent ourselves from making voluntary gestures of the kind described in the previous chapter because they have become a habit with us and are often part of the convention of communication. It would be even more difficult to cure ourselves of involuntary gestures, which are the subject of this chapter, since, as the expression indicates, these are made unintentionally, without our awareness. Through them we reveal our true selves rather than the selves that we would rather show to the world.

An insight into the thoughts, attitudes and feelings of other people is always of value to us, whether this helps us to compete against them more successfully or whether it helps us simply to be more understanding towards them. Knowing what makes someone tick can save a great deal of misunderstanding.

What people don't tell us

Usually a large part of our understanding of other people is gained from what they tell us. This is bound to be somewhat defective since very few people tell everyone in their lives the full truth about themselves. Of course we learn something about them from their actions, and from their background and personal history, but if you want to know something about their inner selves rather than about their public personae you would do well to study the tell-tale signs by which their bodies reveal their personalities.

Involuntary gestures are more difficult to interpret than the voluntary gestures dealt with in the last chapter, mostly because they are less obvious to the untrained eye. If someone is raising a clenched fist at us – a voluntary gesture (*see* page 83) – we are likely to be left in little doubt as to the attitude to us of the person making the gesture. We might not notice, however, that someone to whom we are speaking is constantly clenching and unclenching his or her fists as an unconscious signal of anxiety. Someone standing speaking to someone whose feet are pointing away from us may not realise that that person would rather be gone.

Similarly, if we were late for an appointment with someone and we arrived to find her tapping her feet, it would be abundantly obvious to us that she was annoyed or impatient, or both. But if we were standing speaking to someone whose feet were turned away from us we would be unlikely to pick up on the fact that he or she wished to leave our company unless this fact were obvious from language or facial expression, if we did not know something about body language.

Interpretation

The interpretation of involuntary gestures as part of body language is made more difficult by the fact that, as has been seen above, the involuntary gesture is often saying something completely different from what is being conveyed by other forms of communication, such as speech, facial expressions, gesticulation and voluntary gestures. This is part of the conflict between what someone would like us to believe and what is in fact the true situation, the contrast between the public persona and the private self.

Body Language

How obvious are the involuntary gestures?

To some extent the ease of interpretation of involuntary gestures depends on the degree to which the person concerned uses them and how obvious they are. If someone is nervous, this nervousness is obviously much more difficult to detect if she is simply adjusting a shirt cuff than if she is twisting her hair with one hand and plucking at her skirt with another while at the same time running one foot up and down the back of the other leg. This, of course, sounds like exaggeration, but in some people involuntary gestures do tend to occur in clusters, making it easier to get a picture of the state of mind of the person making the gestures.

Lone gestures

If an involuntary gesture occurs alone and not as part of a cluster, or, indeed, without any backup gesture, it is considerably more difficult to interpret. For example, if there are no other body signals to suggest puzzlement or bewilderment, then someone scratching his head may be doing so simply because his head is itchy rather than because he is secretly indicating that he has a difficult problem to contend with.

Clusters

A body signal can convey a different meaning if it forms part of a cluster. A sitting position involving tightly crossed legs conveys a defensive attitude, but if the person adopting such a position also has his or her head and chin down, then the defensive position becomes one of hostility. Thus it is important to study the whole body rather than to zero in on one body movement or position.

External circumstances

In our zeal to interpret the body language of those around us, we must not forget to take into consideration external circumstances that could affect body movement and position. For example, people at a bus stop may be standing with arms crossed because they are feeling threatened or defensive, or as a sign that they are unconsciously withdrawing from the others in the queue. If it is a very cold day, however, they may be simply standing like that to preserve body heat, particularly if their heads are down and their chins are buried in their chests.

Overlap of gesticulation, voluntary gestures and involuntary gestures

A further difficulty with regard to the study of body

language is the degree of overlap among the various categories that comprise it. We have seen in the previous chapters on gesticulation and voluntary gestures how the same gesture can be categorised under each of these classifications, depending on whether the gesture is accompanied by some form of speech or not. Similarly, some voluntary gestures can be classified also as involuntary gestures if the person who is making the gesture is doing so unconsciously.

The degree of overlap between voluntary gestures and involuntary gestures is nothing like that of the overlap between gesticulation and voluntary gestures, but it should be taken into consideration. Examples include stroking of the chin as a sign of deep thought. This gesture is most often executed by someone unconsciously, but it can be executed by someone quite intentionally to convey the same meaning, often for humorous effect. The gesture is dealt with in detail in the previous chapter on voluntary gestures (*see* page 56).

Another example of a gesture that can be either unconscious or unintentional is that of head-scratching, a sign that the person making the gesture is puzzled or bewildered. When the gesture is intentional it is often used for humorous effect – although, as

has been mentioned above, it can also indicate the
need to relieve an itchy head – and is dealt with in
detail in the previous chapter on voluntary gestures
(*see* page 98).

Signals

The subject of body language, particularly that area
dealing with involuntary gestures, is undoubtedly
quite a complicated one. As has been indicated in
the introduction, however, interpreting a person's
unconscious body signals can be of great use to us in
various areas of our lives. It can be of assistance
when we are buying or selling something, or when
we are interviewing or being interviewed for a job,
or, indeed, in deducing a person's true attitude to us
in a personal relationship. It is thus worth learning
about a few of the signals by which people reveal
themselves to us.

The face

Usually the face is the first part of a person's body
that we notice. Indeed, it is the part by which we recognise people. Partly because it contains the eyes,
which mirror all our emotions, it is the most expressive part of the body. Sometimes, however, facial
expressions do not tell the whole story, or some-

times give the wrong story, and we have to look elsewhere for the true state of someone's feelings or thoughts.

Position of the head during conversation

The head is also of great importance in interpreting someone's body language. If you want to gauge the degree of a person's interest in what you are saying, for example, you would do well to take note of what their head is doing. If the head is in a neutral position, there is little to be deduced, but if the head is tilted to one side then this is a signal that the person's interest has been aroused by our remarks and is an incentive to continue.

Nodding the head

You should be further encouraged if the person involved is giving slight nods, sometimes of an almost imperceptible nature, since these nods indicate an unconscious agreement with what you are saying, or encouragement. Salesmen who have mastered the art of interpreting body signals will be delighted to see these nods as it probably means that they have a good chance of making a sale. A head-nod is often a sign of encouragement from the hearer that the speaker has been met with approval and should continue in the same vein. Head-nodding can, of course, be a conscious gesture, whether as a sign of agreement, acceptance or greeting, and has been dealt with in the chapter on voluntary gestures (*see* page 87).

Shaking the head

The person whom you are engaging in conversation may well not be in agreement with you. Long before this fact is communicated to you in speech, you may spot the odd scarcely perceptible shake of the head, an unconscious gesture made by your hearer to signal non-agreement or discouragement. Salesmen encountering such head-shaking would do well to alter the sales pitch or give up. Like head-nodding, head-shaking can be quite deliberate, whether as a sign of disagreement, refusal or greeting, and has been dealt with in the chapter on voluntary gestures (*see* page 87).

Head and hand position

The neutral head position may not give much away if interpreted on its own. However, the hands are frequently involved in signals involving the head, and so the speaker would do well to take note of the position of his listener's hands. If the listener's head is in a neutral position but his hand is touching his cheek, perhaps rubbing it slightly, then he is subconsciously weighing up what the speaker is saying before coming to a decision. If he is stroking his chin, especially with his thumb and index finger forming a V as he does so, as though making the shape of a beard, then he is thinking deeply about what has been said. The contemplative chin-stroking gesture can also be an

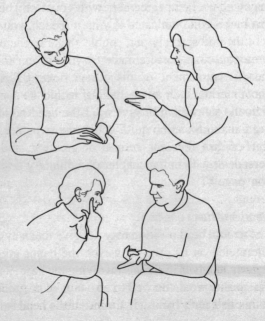

intentional one and has been dealt with in the chapter on voluntary gestures (*see* page 56).

Low head position

If the head of the listener is lowered then he is giving negative signals about what the speaker is saying. This gesture is often part of a gesture cluster, and if the listener's arms are folded it backs up the negativity suggested by the lowered head, since it can be a sign of withdrawal.

Breaking communication

Head movements make for a more flowing form of conversation. They are an indication that the conversation is a two-way thing, even if one person is doing most of the talking. A sudden return to the neutral head position is sometimes an indication that the person who is doing the listening thinks that the conversation that has been taking place should be brought to an end. The gesture is often accompanied by a lowering of the eyes so as to break eye contact and so break communication.

A guide to mood

The position of the head can also be a guide to someone's mood or state of mind. If the head is lowered then it can be an indication that the person is feeling depressed or sad. The depression or sorrow may be short-lived, in which case the gesture will be likewise short-lived. For example, such a position may well be adopted short-term by someone if a good friend or a member of the family has just gone away for a while. On the other hand, someone who routinely feels rather down very often has a more or less permanently lowered head. People suffering from depression often have such a posture.

Signs of submission
It is as well to look for other signs in the presence of a slightly lowered head. It can, of course, be used intentionally as a sign of a formal greeting, but it can also be used subconsciously as a sign of submission, a sign that the person with the lowered head is in the presence of someone whom he considers to be better or more important than he is himself. This information could be of great value to someone engaged in some kind of competition with the person who has involuntarily lowered his head. It could mean that he is feeling one down and so his opponent has a distinct advantage.

A pensive state
The lowered head does not always signify either de-

pressed spirits or feelings of submission or inferiority. Someone who is walking along with the head lowered may well be neither depressed nor feeling inferior. People frequently adopt such a position when they have gone for a walk to think about some problem that is preoccupying them. We have all at some time or other been passed by a friend who was walking along thoughtfully studying the ground.

Tossing the head

The tossing of the head is a gesture that can qualify either as a voluntary gesture or an as an involuntary gesture and has been dealt with fully in the chapter on voluntary gestures (*see* page 88). When the head is tossed unconsciously, it is more likely to be a vain gesture or a sexual come-on rather than the sign of defiance that is the primary significance of the conscious gesture, although the defiant head toss does exist as an involuntary gesture, when the toss is considerably sketchier and so is not so noticeable. Whether it is conscious or not, the gesture is much more likely to be executed by women and girls than men and boys.

As has been indicated above, the head is sometimes used in conjunction with the hands to convey a subconscious reaction. Some gestures using the head and hands are also capable of being voluntary gestures and have been dealt with in the chapter on voluntary gestures.

Head-scratching

These gestures include head-scratching, which indicates that the person doing the scratching is puzzled or bewildered by something, unless the head-scratching is for the relief of an itchy head. Head-scratching as a voluntary gesture is often a camped-up gesture for humorous effect, whereas as an involuntary gesture the scratching is much more minimal. In fact, when the gesture is used subconsciously it can be more of a sketchy head-rubbing than a full-blown head-scratching. If, when someone is giving a talk and several of the audience are to be seen rubbing their heads, then the lecturer's technique needs some improvement.

Head-slapping

These gestures also include head-slapping, a gesture that indicates that the performer of the gesture has suddenly realised that something important has been forgotten or remembered too late, in the same way that slapping the forehead (dealt with below under the brow) does. Head-slapping is more likely than

forehead-slapping to be used as a conscious gesture
and is dealt with in the chapter on voluntary gestures
(*see* page 99). As an involuntary gesture it is again a
more minimal, less obvious one. You may well see
someone who has just got into a car after a trip to the
supermarket making such a gesture. All of us have
had the experience of going out to buy some specific
item and coming out of the shop having bought
practically everything but the said item.

Supporting the head with the hand
If the head is supported by the hand, often executed in
a sitting position with the elbow leaning on a table or
desk, then the person making the gesture may well be
tired. Perhaps the gesture comes at the end of a long
day's work and the head-holder cannot wait to get
home. Alternatively, the person may be extremely
bored rather than tired, although the degree of stultifi-
cation and the degree of desire to go home will be
about the same. Obviously this is one involuntary
gesture that it would be well to gain some control
over. It would never do if the boss had any knowledge
of body language and went in to an office and saw all
his staff with heads supported by hands

The less at ease people are feeling, the more
movements they are likely to make. This being the

case, people who are feeling nervous are likely to touch their heads or their faces with their hands frequently as a subconscious signal of their anxiety or nervousness. Generally speaking, people who are of a nervous or less confident disposition rarely just have their hands quietly at their sides.

Hands clasped behind head
On the other hand, people who are feeling far from nervous but who indeed are ultra-confident also use their heads and hands subconsciously to demonstrate this fact. They clasp their hands behind the backs of their heads and, if they are sitting down, they also lean back on the chair. They are indicating, unlike people who fold their arms, that they have no fear in exposing the front of their bodies, that they

do not feel threatened in any way.

The gesture involving the hands clasped behind the head, which indicates that the person is feeling totally at ease, is one frequently assumed by people in authority. For example, a bank manager may adopt it unconsciously when in the course of an interview with someone who is asking for a loan and so is far from being at ease.

Sometimes people unconsciously mimic the gestures of others. It is by no means unusual to see a group of men, all of equal status and all high in confidence levels, all sitting around making this gesture. Women are much less likely to do so, although they themselves sometimes use the same gesture in other situations. For example, people of either sex may well fold their hands behind their heads if they are taking a break from a piece of work and are feeling pleased and confident with the progress of the work.

Unconscious mimicking

The unconscious mimicking of gestures is not restricted to people who are confidently folding their hands behind their heads. It is very common for people who are involved in a conversation, either a friendly informal conversation or a more formal one, with a high degree of agreement to make the same kind of gestures. Thus you will see them nodding and tilting their heads, and generally making unconscious signals that they are on the same wavelength.

This mirroring of gestures is sometimes noticeable in the general behaviour of people who have known each other for a long time, who are totally at ease with each other, and who are fully aware of each other's attitudes and opinions. If you watch two friends having a good old gossip over a cup of coffee in a café, you will notice that their unconscious gestures are remarkably similar. The concept of mirror gestures is particularly true of couples who have been married for a long time. It is said that they grow to resemble each other physically, but their unconscious gestures certainly grow to resemble each other.

The hair

The hair is, of course, closely associated with the head and is much used in the making of subcon-

scious gestures. When people are feeling nervous or
ill at ease, they frequently touch their hair and reveal
their nerves, even when they otherwise look confident. If you are attending an interview with several
other candidates, all of whom look supremely confident, it is comforting to watch them touching their
hair. Sometimes hair-touching takes the form of frequent hair-grooming, such as the pressing in of
waves, but this can still be a sign of ill-ease rather
than a sign of excessive vanity.

Hair patting and grooming
Patting of the hair and frequent hair-grooming, such
as the pushing back of the hair from the forehead,
generally can be a sign of excessive vanity, carried
out by people who are particularly concerned with
their physical appearance. They are of the kind who
cannot pass a mirror or even a shop window without
looking at their reflections.

Unconscious hair-grooming, including hair-patting and pushing back of the hair, when this is done
in the presence of a member of the opposite sex, can
be a courting signal. Preening, such as hair-patting,
can be the human equivalent of birds fluffing out
their feathers as part of a mating ritual. A group of
young men standing at a street corner with a view

to checking out the local talent will almost certainly put their hands to their hair if a group of girls go by. The girls, if they have any interest in the young men, will almost certainly make similar hair-grooming gestures and may also indulge in a bit of unconscious head-tossing, a gesture dealt with above and in the chapter on voluntary gestures (*see* page 88).

Hair twisting

Hair-twisting is indicative of even greater nervousness than just hair-touching. It is often not just an isolated gesture but part of a habit that is very difficult to break. The gesture is more common among women than men, possibly because they generally have more hair. If you stand in a room where stu-

dents are taking an exam, there is often quite a forest of hands twisting away at hair as the female students read the exam paper. Because of its very nature it is an extremely obvious habit, even more obvious than, say, nail-biting. In the light of this, it is well worth trying to break a habit that is such a giveaway of a nervous state.

Pushing the hair behind the ears
Some people are given to pushing their hair behind their ears and so betray the fact that they are not at ease, although this is sometimes an unconscious preening gesture. Alternatively, they show their nervousness or unease by compulsively rubbing their necks and pushing their hair up off their necks over their heads.

Hair sucking

Another sign of nervousness or anxiety involving the hair is slightly less savoury – that of sucking or chewing the hair. This is, of course, subject to having hair that is long enough to reach the mouth and teeth. As is the case with hair-twisting, this is an unconscious habit that some people, usually women, find it very difficult to wean themselves from. Some chewers of hair claim, and they could well be right, that they make this gesture, not when they are nervous but when they are concentrating. This is an analogy with the possible double interpretation of biting pens or pencils.

Running the fingers through the hair

Running one's fingers through someone else's hair is a romantic gesture. Running one's fingers through one's own hair, however, is a totally different kind

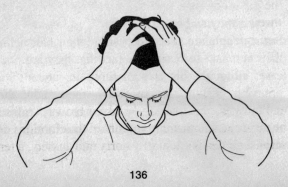

of gesture. It signifies desperation, anger, frustration or some related emotion. For example, people who have just made a mistake in a piece of important work might well run their fingers through their hair. The gesture can also be an intentional one and can even be accompanied by speech.

The brow
The furrowed brow
The furrowed brow can signal a number of emotions, and to interpret these it is necessary to look for other backup signs – for example, the expression in the eyes. Sometimes the correct interpretation depends on the degree of furrowing – for example, a person in a furiously angry mood may have brows more deeply furrowed than the same person in a mildly anxious mood – although this can vary from person to person. The emotions that tend to be signalled by the furrowed brow include anger, anxiety, puzzlement and deep thought. In addition, the brow furrows automatically when gestures involving the raising of the eyebrows, of the kind described below, are made.

Some people furrow their brows so much that they end up with permanently wrinkled brows. This can be put down to an undue amount of the emotions described above, particularly worry and anxiety, a ten-

dency to raise the eyebrows a lot, or it may have a physical cause, such as the person having poor eyesight or being out a lot in strong sunlight.

Placing the hand on the brow
Putting the hand to the brow can be a sign that the person making the gesture is worried or anxious, although it can also be a sign that he or she is tired or, indeed, in pain and has a headache. The gesture can also indicate deep thought, especially if the eyes are downcast and the head lowered. People frequently make this gesture when they are trying to remember something, such as someone's name or where they have put something.

Slapping the brow
When the hand is put to the brow in a slapping movement, rather than just a touching movement,

the significance of the gesture is that the person involved has forgotten something and has either just remembered this or has just had the fact brought to his or her attention. The forehead is subconsciously slapped as being located near the brain, source of the brow-slapper's problem. The slapping of the forehead is similar to the slapping of the back or side of the head, mentioned above under the head (*see* page 128) and dealt with in the chapter on voluntary gestures (*see* page 99). Like head-slapping, it can be a conscious gesture, usually of rather a theatrical kind, but it is more usually an unconscious gesture.

The eyebrows

The eyebrows are a more obvious feature of some faces than others. Some people have great shaggy eyebrows that seem to take up most of their foreheads, while others have rather sparse eyebrows, frequently, in the case of women, carefully trimmed into such sparseness. However bushy or narrow they are, eyebrows play a significant part in the giving of body signals.

Raising or lowering the eyebrows

The raising or lowering of the eyebrows can be categorised both as voluntary gestures and involuntary gestures and are treated in detail in the chapter on voluntary gestures (*see* page 99). The difference between the unintentional and the intentional gesture is simply one of degree, the unintentional version being significantly less obvious and more subtle than the intentional version.

Thus, slightly raised eyebrows indicate that the person making the gesture is surprised or shocked. Eyebrow-raising can be a response, for example, to an act of unconventional behaviour. Because of this, the gesture has come to be used figuratively. Thus we make remarks like, 'There were quite a few raised eyebrows when the boss was seen having dinner with the new secretary,' when, for all we know, no one actually physically raised their eyebrows. The raised eyebrow has simply become a linguistic symbol for surprise or outrage.

People who are displeased, puzzled or worried of-

ten lower their eyebrows. This lowering can vary in degree, sometimes being so slight as to manifest itself only in a very slight furrowing of the brows. If you spot this body signal in the boss it is time to mend your ways – its presence indicates that either you or your work is causing irritation

Eyebrow-flashing

Eyebrow-flashing occurs when, as an unconscious greeting, someone raises the eyebrows for a fraction of a second. It is a friendly signal that occurs spontaneously when we make visual contact with someone whom we know and like, or with someone whom we do not know but would like to know. Usually accompanied by a smile, it is body language for a brief welcome. For example, people spotting friends or acquaintances across a room will automatically perform the eyebrow-flashing gesture.

The eyes

The eyes play a very important part in a person's features, and they also play an important role in body language.

A genuine smile

For example, the eyes are an indication as to the

genuineness of someone's smile. The false smile, for whatever reason it is assumed, is all too familiar a part of our society, but the eyes usually give it away. The person intent on giving a social smile may turn up the lips in the appropriate gesture associated with smiling, and may even narrow and crinkle the eyes as people do in a real smile, but it is almost impossible to make the eyes light up with genuine warmth, pleasure and happiness in the way they do in a genuine, spontaneous smile.

Sorrow and sadness

Sorrow and sadness are indicated by the eyes. This is transmitted not only by the miserable expression in the eyes but sometimes by the fact that they are filled with tears. Even when people are trying to put a brave face on things and pretend not to be sad or hurt, their eyes can give them away if tears form in them, however minimally. In the same way, tears can form in the eyes of people who are in great pain, even although they may be shrugging off the pain.

Interpretation of mood

Obviously, eye expressions are important to us in our interpretation of the mood of others We have seen above that they can express happiness and sadness, but they can also express amusement, anger, love, fear, surprise, fatigue, and so on. Some emotions cause us literally and unconsciously to open our eyes wider. Such a gesture, which can also be used as a rather theatrical conscious gesture, tends to be an unconscious reaction to surprise or shock, and could occur, for example, if you opened the door to see standing there an old friend whom you had not seen for a long time and whom you were not expecting. Our habit of opening our eyes wide is reflected in the language. When you learn of something that surprises you greatly you can describe it as 'a real eye-opener'.

Eye contact
We can learn something about people from their eye contact with each other. People in the course of a conversation look at each other frequently. How long the

contact lasts obviously varies, but the length of time it lasts can be an indication of how well the people involved know each other. In the case of strangers it can be very short indeed, and in the case of lovers it is likely to be very long – that between good friends lies somewhere in between. When two people hold eye contact slightly longer than normal then this is often a sign that they are feeling sexually or romantically attracted to each other.

How often people make eye contact in the course of a conversation varies as well as does the length of contact. Again, how well they know each other tends to have some bearing on this, and people tend to look at the other person more often when they are listening than they do when they are doing the talking.

There is a general feeling around that people who cannot look you straight in the face are untrustworthy or have something to hide. Certainly it is the case that people making minimal eye contact with their partner in conversation are likely to be indicating some negative attitude, but this need not necessarily be sinister. They can be lying or they can be committing some act of dishonesty, but they may just be shy or easily intimidated. People also tend not to look at someone very much when the subject is one that causes distress.

There are cultural differences associated with eye contact. Japanese people, for example, usually avoid direct eye contact as part of their culture, whilst members of the Arab peoples tend to use eye contact far more than we do in our Western culture.

Thus it is clear that we should not too readily assume that someone who is avoiding eye contact is shifty, dishonest or unreliable. In addition, the association between avoidance of eye contact and dishonesty is too well known, and forcing oneself to make regular eye contact is too easy to do, so that people who are intent on deceiving you can look you straight in the eye and go on deceiving you.

If, in the course of a conversation, you realise that the other person is not making eye contact with you for any length of time but keeps swerving the eyes away and making rapid glances from side to side, it could be because he or she is not finding you very interesting or attractive and is unconsciously looking out for someone whom they think they will find more so. You should not be too downhearted if you spot such signals. They could be caused not by boredom but by nervousness or by the fact that the person is lying. People who are exceptionally nervous not only show this by the rapid glances just de-

scribed but sometimes by a rapid opening and clos-
ing of the eyes.

If the person who is not making eye contact with
you is staring into the air, you have more cause for
concern. There is highly likely to be a marked degree of boredom in this gesture. On the other hand,
if he or she is staring at the ground this may be an
indication of some kind of submission, of the kind
that might accompany feelings of guilt, although it
can be simply a sign of contemplation and that your
partner in conversation is thinking deeply about
something.

Staring

Making regular eye contact is one thing; staring is
something else. As children we are taught that it is
rude to stare, and certainly if we know that people
are staring at us we feel embarrassed and uncomfortable. If you are having a conversation with
someone and that person is staring at you, it can be a
sign that he or she is trying to dominate you or exercise some kind of authority over you.

If someone is staring, not at a partner in conversation but at someone or something else, this is an indication that the person is surprised or amazed by
what has been seen. Should the person be staring,

not at someone or something but into space, then he or she is either lost in thought or is daydreaming.

Eye-rubbing

We have seen above how people frequently touch parts of their faces or heads when they are nervous, when they are feeling some doubt about what is being said, or when they are lying. This is as true of the eyes as it is of other parts of the face and head. Sometimes the eyes are touched, sometimes rubbed, although eye-rubbing is also a traditional sign that the person making the gesture is tired. Children in particular often make such a gesture when they are feeling sleepy.

Shutting the eyes

People frequently shut their eyes briefly when they are tired, but the same gesture can suggest boredom. It is really a sign that someone wants to shut out the world for a while and can be a signal of exasperation or frustration. A similar gesture is that of putting one's hands over one's eyes, which is dealt with in the chapter on voluntary gestures (*see* page 102).

Half-shut eyes are sometimes associated with sexual passion. Certainly, steamy love scenes in films are apt to portray such expressions on the faces of the relevant characters. Half-shut eyes, however, can sometimes be a sign of something more mundane. Narrowed eyes can be a sign of anger, or a sign that someone is attempting to remember something that has been forgotten, such as a telephone number.

Looking under the eyelashes
Looking under the eyelashes at someone is a gesture usually associated with the female of the species. It can suggest modesty or shyness, but it is often more of a flirtatious gesture or a sexual come-on.

Winking
Winking at someone is also often a sexual gesture, although it can also be indicative of secrecy or confidentiality. Unless it is a nervous tic, however, winking is generally a conscious gesture and so is dealt with in the chapter on voluntary gestures (*see* page 105).

The cheeks
Stroking the cheeks
Cheeks also feature in body language. People who stroke their cheeks subconsciously are very possibly in a thoughtful mood. They are either trying to weigh

up a situation or a person, or trying to solve a problem, as is the case in Britain at least, but in some other European countries, such as Greece, Italy or Spain, the gesture is made by males to express their admiration of an attractive girl or woman.

Worry

As has already been mentioned, people who are of a less confident disposition tend to make more body movements than their more confident counterparts. People who continually touch their cheeks may be in a state of anxiety. For example, a hostess at a dinner party may be doing her best to appear happy, but if her fingers are frequently in contact with her cheek then she is very possibly worrying about something. She could be concerned in case the soufflé for dessert has fallen or she could be worrying because one of her children has not returned at the expected time. In either event, however competently she is dealing with the conversational gambits, at least part of her mind is elsewhere.

The ears

Rubbing the ear lobe

It is not only the cheek that the nervous keep touching in moments of stress. Some rather nervous or anxious people unconsciously finger their ear lobes You may find yourself having to make a journey by air with a colleague. If he or she is sitting in the departure lounge feverishly rubbing an ear lobe then it is a distinct possibly that your colleague is afraid of flying. If the colleague is a woman she may be twiddling an earring rather than fingering an ear lobe.

Touching the rim of the ear
Another ear gesture that is indicative of nervousness is that of running a finger rhythmically up and down the outward edge of the ear. Some people of an anxious temperament are so addicted to this unconscious habit that they end up with a permanently red ear.

Ear-touching is open to another interpretation. It can be a signal not so much of nervousness or anxiety but of uneasiness caused by the fact that the ear-twiddler has doubts about the truth of what a speaker is saying. A salesperson spotting this gesture in a potential customer should modify the sales spiel as it clearly lacks conviction. On the other hand, ear-touching can be a sign that the person making the gesture is himself lying.

Covering the ears with the hands
Another unconscious gesture involving the ear is

the covering of the ears with the hands. This can occur in moments of stress, as though the person making the gesture is desirous of shutting out what is happening around him or her and wishes to switch off. People covering their ears with their hands are shutting out the world rather than just shutting out local noise and may make the gesture at the end of a series of disasters or misfortunes, as though unconsciously indicating that it is the last straw.

Covering the ears with the hands is one of the gestures that are dealt with in the chapter on voluntary gestures (*see* page 105). As a conscious gesture people use it to shut out noise or to indicate their dislike of some sound. A more minimal form of this can be an example of an involuntary gesture, having the same significance as the intentional gesture. Thus, if you cover your ears with your hands you can be shutting out unwanted sounds or noise, or shutting out the world in general.

Putting fingers in the ears
Another ear gesture that is indicative of a desire to shut out noise is that of sticking one's fingers in one's ears. This gesture is usually an intentional one and as such has been dealt with in the chapter on

voluntary gestures (*see* page 104). An unconscious version of this occurs when a person screws a finger backwards and forwards inside the ear, signalling that the person has heard enough of what is going on around him or her, or of what someone is saying to him or her. It may mean that he or she is tired of being the listener and wishes to have a turn at speaking. A similar gesture with much the same significance occurs when someone keeps bending the entire ear over the ear hole, as though to exclude all sound or what is going on around him or her. Yet another version of this is the rubbing of the whole ear or even simply the rubbing of the back of the ear.

The nose

As with other features of the face, the nose is used in body language. Some gestures involving the nose have been treated in the chapter on voluntary gestures (*see* page 52). Of these, nose-wrinkling is a common unconscious gesture.

Nose wrinkling

Signifying distaste or displeasure, the gesture is often barely perceptible, but since it is an important indicator as to how someone is reacting or responding to something or someone, it is one that is well worth looking out for. As a voluntary gesture the wrinkled nose is often an indication that someone has detected the presence of an unpleasant smell, although it can also be a sign of distaste or disapproval.

Holding the nostrils

Holding the nostrils closed is also a voluntary gesture used to signify the presence of an unpleasant smell. This gesture requires such a definite action that it is unlikely to be an involuntary gesture. There are other nose gestures, however, that are performed quite unconsciously. These include the scratching, rubbing or touching of the nose. Since this is capable of more than one interpretation, those wishing to find out what it conveys in a particular situation should look for other backup gestures to confirm their interpretation.

Rubbing or touching the nose

They should consider the possibility that the person doing the nose-rubbing or nose-touching, or indeed the touching of the part of the face below the nose and above the mouth, is in fact lying. In the same way that children often put their hands to their mouths when lying, or when they have been found out in a lie, so do many adults touch some part of their face or head when they are not telling the whole truth.

People sometimes scratch the nose when they are puzzled, as others might scratch the head in similar circumstances, but people also put their hands to their noses when they are feeling uncertain or uneasy. These feelings of unease are often caused by the fact that they suspect someone who is speaking of not telling the truth. As is described below, chin-touching as well as nose-touching can also indicate a lack of belief in what is being said.

Thus nose-touching can signify lying or the suspicion that someone else is lying. In addition, it can, like other forms of face-touching, be a signal that someone is feeling nervous or anxious. This habit of putting one's hands to the face or head has been described above.

The nose gestures that have just been described should not be confused with the gesture of nose-tapping as a voluntary gesture, dealt with in the previous chapter and indicating secrecy or confidentiality (*see* page 52). This is used, for example, when someone is telling someone else a piece of juicy gossip that they should not pass on – although they probably will.

The mouth

The mouth, lips and tongue are of central importance

in speech. Although their role in body language is not quite so important, partly because there are far more body parts involved in body language than there are in speech, they still play a significant part.

Yawning

The mouth plays an important part in facial expressions, such as smiling or grimacing, but it is also the part of the body used in yawning. Yawning is a sign that people are either tired or bored and is a gesture that can be made quite intentionally. As such it has been dealt with in the chapter on voluntary gestures (*see* page 62). It can also be an involuntary gesture with the same meaning, although it is often a more suppressed form of the action. People have been conditioned to cover their mouths with their hands when they yawn as an act of politeness. They thus tend to raise their hands subconsciously to cover up the least obvious of yawns. If you see a hand creeping towards the mouth of your listener it would be as well to cut your comments short.

An open mouth

An open mouth need not signify a yawn. It is a classic unconscious reaction to hearing or seeing something that is very surprising or shocking. For example, if two people who have always seemed to loathe each other suddenly decide to get married, the news is likely to leave their friends with open mouths to a greater or lesser degree. The gesture is sometimes referred to figuratively in the language. For example, someone might say, 'We were all open-mouthed when he left all that money – we thought he was penniless.' This does not necessarily indicate that everyone physically had their mouths open but simply that they were very surprised.

Covering the mouth with the hands

We have seen above how children sometimes cover their mouths when they lie and how adults sometimes touch their noses, ears or chins when they are lying. Another possible indication of lying is a gesture involving several fingers covering the mouth with the thumb against the cheek, a less obvious form of the full hand over the mouth, although, in fact, the full hand version is occasionally used by adult liars as well as by more junior ones.

Placing the fingers in the mouth

If the fingers are placed not over the mouth but in the mouth, it is a sign not of deceit but of insecurity or a sign that the person making the gesture is under

some form of stress or pressure. It is the adult version of the young child sucking the thumb for comfort, a gesture thought to be an unconscious attempt to revert to the comfort and security of sucking the mother's breast. As an alternative to putting the fingers in the mouth, some people put a variety of objects, such as pens or pencils, in their mouths, and smokers, of course, use pipes, cigars or cigarettes

The lips
The lips are the most outwardly important part of the mouth. Their importance in body language has already been discussed in the previous chapter on voluntary gestures, where lip-licking and kiss-blowing are discussed (*see* page 50).

Licking the lips

Lip-licking as an intentional gesture is an anticipatory gesture of something pleasant, particularly something pleasant to eat. This gesture in a more minimal way can also be an example of an involuntary gesture. It, too, can be an anticipatory body signal, but the licking or the wetting of the lips as an unconscious gesture is often indicative of sexual attraction. People at parties, for example, may well be seen almost imperceptibly wetting their lips if they are introduced to people of the opposite sex whom they would like to get to know better. When the lip-wetting is very obvious and unconscious it can be a sign of a lascivious person, someone from whom members of the opposite sex often recoil automatically.

The tongue

The tongue is well known as a sign of rudeness, although sticking out one's tongue to insult people is almost always the province of children, unless adults are making such a gesture for humorous effect. Obviously, this gesture is an intentional one and has been dealt with in the chapter on voluntary gestures (*see* page 91). As an unconscious gesture, sticking the tongue out slightly between the teeth

signifies great concentration. Again, this is a habit much associated with children, but adults, particularly adults who are engaged in some kind of work that they are not used to, also reveal their concentration by such a gesture but in a less obvious form.

The teeth

As has been described above, the teeth are sometimes used with the tongue in a gesture indicative of concentration.

Chewing

They are also used to chew pens or pencils in a gesture denoting concentration or thought but also sometimes denoting nervousness or tension. Most parents will at some time or other have taken a well-chewed pencil from a schoolbag. Some people chew gum a lot, and this can be a sign of nervousness or tension, although it can be just a habit. Other people reveal their nervousness or tension by making an unconscious and compulsive chewing gesture with their teeth.

Biting the nails

Of course the teeth are not only used to chew pens, pencils and like objects. As has been mentioned above in the comments on hair, nervous people sometimes show their uneasiness by chewing on the ends of the hair. Teeth play a major part in one of the most common nervous habits of all, that of finger-nail biting. Some people, whenever they are nervous or under stress, will immediately put their fingers to their mouths and start chewing feverishly. It is one of the few body signals that quite a few people, mainly women, succeed in overcoming, simply because bitten nails are not an attractive attribute and certainly do not benefit from the application of nail varnish.

Clenched teeth

Teeth, then, can be used in conjunction with other parts of the body, or other objects, to give body signals, but they can also be used on their own. Often when people are just hanging on to their tempers and no more, they clench their teeth in an effort to control their rage. Thus, we often hear of someone speaking through clenched teeth when he or she would love to explode but has, for some reason, to go on acting and speaking in a less passionate, more reasoned way.

The chin

Chins are not left out of the body-language picture. Chin-stroking has been referred to above in the context of the neutral head position (*see* page 120). As has been described, it is a sign of deep thought, but it can also be a sign of admiration. The gesture is more often made by men than women, and the object of their admiration can be either a member of the opposite sex or something dear to their hearts, such as a particular kind of car.

Stroking the chin

The chin gesture just mentioned consists of the stroking of the chin with the thumb and index finger, a gesture making a representation of a beard. This gesture suggests contemplation, but simple chin-rubbing is expressive of doubt rather than contemplation. If you think you are doing well in some sales pitch or in some other form of speech or conversation and your listener suddenly embarks on chin-rubbing, then think again. The truth of what you are saying is being challenged.

Cupping the chin

If someone is sitting with the chin and jaw cupped in a hand with the fingers resting along the cheek in an attitude along the lines of the pose of Rodin's statue entitled *The Thinker*, it is a sign that the person is lost in deep contemplation. If both hands are involved in supporting the chin then thinking is still a possible interpretation, but the interpreter of body language will have to look for other signs or read what the eyes are saying to decide what the gesture means. The chin cupped in two hands can also be a

sign that the person indulging in the gesture is feeling downcast.

Protruding chin

If the chin and jaw are unconsciously protruding, and this is not just an anatomical feature, then it can be a sign that the person concerned is in a determined and aggressive mood or is of a determined and aggressive personality. Sometimes the action is an indication that the person is feeling defensive and so is overcompensating.

Receding chin

When the chin and jaw are tucked into the neck it is a sign of lack of confidence and of reticence. It is as though the people involved are retreating as far as possible into themselves, so unsure of themselves are they. This gesture can be very revealing, as it sometimes conflicts with the confident words that are being uttered.

The neck

Sticking the neck out

The neck also has its due share of body signals. People who often perform a gesture consisting of sticking their necks out and then pulling them in, sometimes at the same time adjusting their collars, are often signalling anxiety or nervousness. You can sometimes spot people being interviewed on television and, understandably nervous, making this gesture.

Touching the neck
Touching the neck, as is the case with touching parts of the face and head, can be a sign that the person involved is feeling uncomfortable and could well be lying. If, however, the person is actually clasping the back of the neck with a hand, it can be a sign of anger unless the person involved has a sore neck that he is nursing. It is as well to learn how to interpret the neck clasp since you can take appropriate action and avoid the next stage, which can be a towering rage.

Slapping the neck
Slapping the neck, unlike clasping the neck, is usually a sign that the person making the gesture has just remembered something that should not have been forgotten and is slapping himself in annoyance. Of course, he could be swatting a mosquito that has just bitten him.

Scratching the neck
When the index finger scratches the neck repeatedly just below the ear lobe or scratches the side of the neck it is frequently a sign that the maker of the gesture is feeling unsure or uncertain and expressing silent doubts. This gesture, as is the case with other unconscious gestures of doubt, is frequently manifested by someone who is verbally expressing agreement with, or acceptance of, something that has been said, and so the body signal and spoken message are contradictory.

Tugging at the collar
If someone is wearing a collar, particularly if the person in question is a male, and is feeling nervous he may well run his hand along between the collar and his neck, pulling or tugging at the collar so as to relieve the effects of being hot. It is the kind of ges-

ture that might be made by a bridegroom waiting at the altar for his bride. The gesture need not express nerves but some kind of discomfort or unease. For example, someone who is feeling embarrassed or guilty may make the collar-pulling gesture.

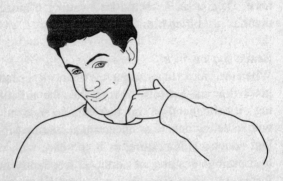

The shoulder shrug

As a conscious gesture the shoulder-shrug, dealt with in the chapter on voluntary gestures (*see* page 71), can signify either a lack of knowledge or information about something or a feeling of indifference. Scarcely perceptible versions of these exist as involuntary gestures with much the same meaning, with perhaps a greater leaning towards indifference. If you are looking for enthusiastic volunteers it is worth keeping a close eye on the shoulders of your intended victims.

The arms

The arms are much used in body language. Expansive, outgoing people tend to use their arms a great deal in the course of conversation. Some of this arm movement is conscious, as when people are using their arms to help them describe something, but some of it is unintentional and is simply a part of their extrovert personalities. More reserved people tend to keep their arms closer to their bodies.

We have seen in the previous chapter on voluntary gestures that the arms feature a great deal in the making of conscious gestures, and these have been dealt with in detail there. Such gestures include arm-waving, which can signify either a greeting, an attempt to indicate one's presence and attract attention, or a warning to keep away (*see* page 68). By their very nature these gestures are unlikely to be made unconsciously. Obviously, most people would notice if they were waving their arms around.

Arms akimbo

The gesture, known as 'arms akimbo', a gesture made by placing the hands on the hips and bending out the elbows in a kind of triangular shape, and most frequently performed by a member of the female sex, signifies anger or aggression, being imitative of a bird fluffing up its feathers to make it seem bigger and so more threatening. The gesture is often executed as a conscious gesture, being dealt with in the chapter on voluntary gestures (*see* page 93). However, it can be a habit that people turn to quite unconsciously when they are in a temper and feeling aggressive.

A one-armed version of the 'arms akimbo', in which only one hand rests on the side, or more usually on the hip, can also signify anger. A gesture made mainly by women and girls, it can be made quite intentionally and is dealt with under voluntary gestures (*see* page 94). It can also be made totally unconsciously, as a reaction to something or someone that has annoyed the person making the gesture.

As well as signifying anger, the hand on hip can be indicative of a sexual come-on, as the gesture shows off the figure to advantage, if you have the right kind of figure, of course. The hand on the hip can also be an indication that the person making the gesture is rather a vain person, given to showing off her figure.

Crossing or folding the arms

As has been indicated above, people who are of a reticent disposition tend to keep their arms close to their bodies. People who go one further cross or fold their arms. This is a defensive, withdrawn position, at the opposite end of the scale from that of the open expansive person who throws the arms wide. Some people claim that they fold their arms simply because they find it a comfortable position, but there is usually more to it than that, and people viewing a set of folded arms tend to get negative vibes.

People who stand, sit or go around with folded arms are subconsciously indicating that they wish to create some kind of barrier between themselves and what is going on around them. Subconsciously they are protecting the front of their bodies against attack and are, for some reason or other, adopting a defensive position. Perhaps they feel threatened in some way by someone or something; perhaps they unconsciously wish to shut themselves off from a set of undesirable circumstances; perhaps they are experiencing negative thoughts about someone with whom they are in contact, or perhaps they are just feeling generally uneasy. People who are feeling insecure or nervous tend to touch themselves a lot – people who are feeling very insecure wrap their arms around themselves.

There are varying degrees of arm-folding – they can be folded loosely or they can be folded extremely tightly. Usually the degree of tightness reflects the strength of the feelings that cause the arm-folding. If someone is feeling threatened and uneasy to an exceptional degree, then the arm-folding will be extremely tight; if someone is feeling only vaguely uneasy then the arm-folding will be of a much looser, more relaxed kind. If the people intent on folding their arms are wearing coats or jackets they pull these tight, a gesture that reinforces their barrier and their feelings of insecurity.

Arm-folding has already been dealt with in the previous chapter on voluntary gestures (*see* page 97), but arm-folding executed as a conscious gesture is usually a gesture caused by anger. Although this is a possibility in the case of subconscious gestures, it is only one possible interpretation and a less common one than those mentioned above.

There is, of course, a physical reason for people folding their arms. In extreme cold they give themselves a self-hug to conserve body temperature and keep themselves warm, and so, before you assume that someone is of a reticent disposition or in a defensive mood, check the temperature.

Folded arms and clenched hands

When the person doing the arm-folding or arm-crossing has clenched fists, and possibly also clenched teeth, he or she may be feeling defensive or withdrawn, but this emotion is accompanied by a feeling of hostility, the clenched fist as a conscious gesture being a sign of aggression or intimidation. The combination of folded arms and clenched hands indicates that there is a potential attacking element in the person making the body signal. He or she is not about to take things lying down.

Folded arms with the thumbs turned up
If the person making the arm-folding or arm-crossing gesture has the thumbs turned up, then it is a signal that, although the person may feel that he is in a defensive position and feel the need of protecting himself, he is also rather self-confident. Generally it is a sign that he has made up his mind and is intent on defending his point of view. The thumbs-up sign as a conscious gesture is a sign of acceptance or approval, or a sign that everything is all right, and is dealt with in detail in the previous chapter on voluntary gestures (*see* page 75).

Folded arms with arms being gripped
Sometimes you see people with arms crossed in such a way that each hand grips the other arm. This is a sign that the people are feeling particularly defensive and probably threatened or frightened, the

hand-gripping being a reinforcement of the defensive signal given out by the crossed arms. People who are afraid of the dentist may well adopt such a position when sitting in the waiting room

A partial crossing of the arms

A partial folding or crossing of the arms or the holding of one arm with the other hand is a less noticeable gesture, and the person making the gesture will not be feeling so defensive, threatened or nervous as the person making the full-blown version. However, this is just a question of degree, and people making the more minimal gesture are still feeling defensive and lacking in self-confidence in the situation in which they find themselves. You may well spot this gesture in some members of a group of people waiting to be interviewed for a job.

The arm that has been placed across the body to touch the other arm has subconsciously formed a barrier, as though to protect the maker of the gesture from what is going on. This protective, rather

nervous crossover gesture can involve a watch or shirt cuff rather than the other arm and is a gesture frequently made by people who are being interviewed on television.

Defensive folding of the arms

As we have seen above, people tend to touch parts of the face when they are lying as well as when they are feeling nervous or insecure. In much the same way, people tend to fold or cross their arms when they are lying, and this should be taken into consideration if you are trying to interpret the gesture. It is possible that people who have crossed their arms have done so as a form of advance, anticipatory defence against a possible challenge to their lies. Such an interpretation of arm-crossing is all the more likely to be accurate if the legs are crossed as well. By making both these gestures the people who are doing so are increasing the unconscious barriers that they have created between themselves and others.

Arms hanging loosely at the sides

People who do not enfold their upper bodies with their arms but have them hanging loosely at their sides are exhibiting a sense of being at ease. They are subconsciously exposing the front of their bodies because they are not afraid of being attacked. This feeling of ease and confidence is underlined further when they hold their arms behind their backs with hands grasped, the palm of one hand gripping the back of the other hand, a gesture that is usually adopted by males. Such a gesture often denotes superiority or authority as well as confidence and is one that is often adopted by male members of royalty and other figures of authority, such as headmasters.

This same feeling of confidence and ease is exhibited by people who put their arms up and place their hands behind heads. This gesture has been described above in the comments on the head.

Arms wide open

Folding or crossing the arms is a tight, closed-in gesture. The opposite of this is a gesture that involves the flinging of the arms wide, a conscious gesture indicating that the relevant person is innocent of all knowledge or involvement, and a subconscious indication that there is nothing to hide and nothing from which the front of the body needs to be shielded. This body signal is dealt with in detail in the chapter on gesticulation.

The hands

Hands, of course, play an important role in body language. Many gestures involving hands relate to conventional greetings or other similar body signals. These include hand-waving to signal goodbye, hand-shaking to signal hello in rather a formal way, and hand-clapping as a signal of public appreciation. Such gestures are made intentionally, and these, and others, are dealt with in the chapter on voluntary gestures.

Clasping the hands

By their very nature, body signals involving hands tend to involve other parts of the body also, but some are restricted to hands. A hands-only gesture occurs when people clasp their hands together in such a way that they look as though they are holding hands with themselves. This is a signal that the people making the gesture are feeling nervous and insecure, and are seeking security of the kind that they once had as children, when they held hands with their parents.

Wringing the hands

One degree further on from this is a gesture known as wringing of the hands, when the hands are together but are in constant motion. Such a gesture denotes a high degree of nervous tension or anxiety. Someone who is petrified of flying but who has been forced to make a trip by air might make this gesture, hands carefully placed in his or her lap in an unconscious attempt to keep the hand-wringing suppressed, and so the nervousness.

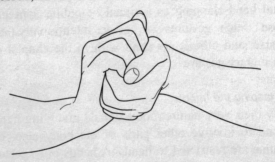

Rubbing the hands

Hand-rubbing, a gesture made by rubbing the palms of the hands round and round each other, is usually a voluntary gesture. As such it is either an anticipatory gesture or a gesture denoting extreme cold and has been dealt with in the chapter on voluntary gestures (*see* page 48). However, a less extreme, less obvious version of this is sometimes used unconsciously. For example, someone anticipating making a handsome profit from some business venture might subconsciously make a more minimal form of the hand-rubbing gesture.

Clenched hands

Clenched hands, like clenched teeth, are a sign of tension of some kind, a sign that the clencher of the hands is practising some kind of restraint. Perhaps the person is very angry and is trying hard not to lose control; perhaps the person is feeling very frustrated and is trying not to make this frustration obvious to others; or perhaps the person is experiencing great pain or unhappiness but has been brought up not to show such feelings. Someone, for example, who has been injured or wounded and is having a wound dressed may well clench his or her hands rather then cry out. Often clenched hands, which are indicative of the range of feelings just described, are placed in the lap out of sight of other people.

If you are engaged in a conversation with someone who otherwise seems to be agreeing with you but who has clenched hands, then the likelihood is that he or she has a negative attitude to you or to the point of view that you are putting forward. In this case the hand-clencher will be more likely to have the hands on view, although the height of the clenched hands can vary. Sometimes the clenched hands will be placed on the desk, sometimes they will be placed in front of the face. Both of these gestures are, like folded arms, forming a barrier between the person making the gesture and the other person taking part in the conversation. The higher

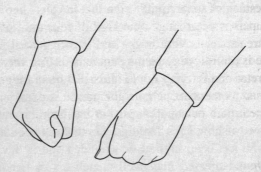

the hands, the greater the barrier and the greater the degree of the negative feelings.

Hand-steepling

Another hand gesture that does not rely on other parts of the body to convey its body signal is hand-steepling or finger-steepling. This gesture is made by putting the hands together, placing the fingertips of each hand together and thereby forming a shape like a church steeple. This gesture can give the appearance of contemplation, particularly when the steepled hands are placed next to the lips, but it is essentially a gesture of superiority in a

superior/subordinate situation. It is the kind of gesture that you might find a headmaster making when he is pontificating on a disagreement over the interpretation of a school rule. This gesture is frequently used by someone who is talking, the kind of speech used often being of a patronising nature, along the lines of, 'Well, well, we'll have to think about that.'

The lowered hand steeple

The gesture described above could be described as a raised steeple. An alternative form of it is the lowered steeple. In this the hands form the shape but the fingers are facing downwards rather than

upwards. The lowered steeple gesture is more likely to be adopted by someone who is listening rather than by someone who is speaking. This gesture can often be construed as being a positive response to what is being heard. However, such a gesture is often the final one in a series of gestures, one occurring towards the end of a conversation, and it tends to take its colour from the gestures leading up to it. Thus, if it follows on from a series of other positive gestures, such as slight nods of the head or a tilted head, then the user of the gesture is most likely making a positive response. If the steeple gesture follows on from a series of negative gestures, such as nose-rubbing or arm-folding, then the user of the gesture is most likely to be making a negative response.

The steeple gesture, particularly the lowered form, can be an evaluative one, performed while the person is weighing up the situation before opting for a positive or negative response. This element of evaluation is most likely to be present in the gesture if the fingers of the hands making the steeple are constantly parting and coming together again.

Hands pressed together
A gesture involving the hands that is similar in some

ways to steepling is one in which someone presses
the hands close together with fingers and palms flat
against each other. Such a gesture indicates that the
person who is making the gesture is emphasising a
point, probably in an attempt to persuade someone
else of the truth of this point.

Fingers intertwined
The most seemingly relaxed hands gesture is
probably that in which hands are folded with
fingers intertwined, the hands being usually placed
in the lap or on a table or other surface. This is a
gesture that is much encouraged in young children,
particularly in children in the classroom, probably
in an effort to make active, mischievous children
sit still for a time and put their hands where the
teacher can see them. In adults the gesture, most
frequently seen in the
female sex, suggests not
relaxation but conven-
tionality or even prim-
ness. Someone sitting
with hands demurely
placed in the lap is
undoubtedly displaying
tendencies to toe the line.

Hands placed behind the head

A gesture that involves the hands but also involves the head is one in which the hands are placed behind the head. This signifies the fact that the person making the gesture is feeling very confident and possibly rather arrogant. This gesture is described above in the comments on body signals involving the head (*see* page 130). People clasping their hands behind their backs are likewise feeling confident and at ease. This gesture is described above in the comments on body signals involving the arms (*see* page 179).

Hands supporting the jaw

Another gesture involving the hands also involves the chin and jaw. This gesture, which can signify either contemplation or a downcast state of mind, is dealt with above under chin (*see* page 162). A similar gesture, also dealt with under chin, involves the chin and the jaw being supported by one hand and denotes deep thought (*see* page 162). When the head, rather than the chin, is supported by a hand, then it is an indication of fatigue or boredom, a gesture dealt with in the comments on gestures involving the head (*see* page 129).

Hands and hips

There are two gestures involving hands and the hips. One is the gesture known as 'arms akimbo' and the other is a one-arm version of these. Both of these are referred to above in the comments on arms (*see* page 167) and are dealt with in detail in the chapter on voluntary gestures (*see* page 93).

The fingers

Pointing and wagging the index finger

The two most important body signals involving only the fingers are pointing the index finger, for example to indicate the location of something, and wagging the finger, for example to admonish someone. Both these are usually intentional gestures accompanied by speech and are dealt with in the chapter on gesticulation (*see* page 30). The pointing finger is, however, by no means unknown as a subconscious gesture in body language. Someone who is making a point in a very angry or aggressive way may well point a finger at the person to whom he is making the point, frequently making jabbing movements with the pointing finger for extra emphasis. People who regularly make this kind of gesture are very often people of rather a dominant or authoritarian personality.

Touching

The fingers often play a part in body language in conjunction with other parts of the body. As has been mentioned earlier, many people, particularly those of a nervous disposition or those who are feeling uneasy for some reason, frequently touch parts of themselves, often those parts that are on or near the face. Such gestures, although they also involve the fingers or hands, have been dealt with in the comments on the other relevant part of the body, such as nose-tapping at nose (*see* page 152) and ear-rubbing at ear (*see* page 149).

Fingers showing nervousness

Two important body signals involving the fingers include the biting of the fingernails, a sign of nervousness or anxiety, and the putting of the fingers in the mouth, a sign of nervousness or feelings of insecurity. These are dealt with above under teeth and the mouth respectively (*see* pages 154 and 159). Some people display their nervousness or unease not by biting their fingernails but by looking at them very carefully. Such a gesture may be a signal of boredom rather than of nervousness, as though the person concerned has nothing better to do.

Fingers are much used in touching of parts of the

body, especially those parts on the face or head. However, they are also used as part of body language to touch objects. For example, someone who is nervous or ill at ease may use his or her fingers to reveal the feelings by twirling the stem of a wineglass in the hands, tapping a cigarette on the table, or constantly rearranging the cutlery at the dinner table. People ill at ease may also use their fingers to pick imaginary pieces of fluff from their jackets or sweaters and make any number of other gestures.

Open palms

We have seen in the chapter on gesticulation that people frequently throw their arms wide with palms upward when they wish to disclaim all knowledge or responsibility for something. The open palms in such a situation are associated with openness, and

this kind of openness is also expressed by open palms in subconscious gestures. If you see someone with his or hands open like this, then you can probably assume that he or she is telling the truth and has nothing to hide, although you should bear in mind that people who make a living by deceiving other people often learn to control their subconscious gestures as well as their conscious gestures and speech. That is why some conmen are so successful.

The thumb

The thumb's role in body language with reference to intentional gestures or gesticulation has been dealt with in the chapter on voluntary gestures (*see* page 75). These include the thumbs-up gesture, denoting that everything is all right, and the classic hitchhiking gesture. Its role in conjunction with folded arms as an involuntary gesture has been described above in the comments on arms (*see* page 171), but it has other roles.

Thumb twiddling

We tend to think of thumb-twiddling, the constant rolling of the thumbs round each other, as a sign of boredom or impatience, or a sign that someone has nothing else to do. Indeed, it has come to be used

figuratively in the language, indicating that someone has been left with nothing to do or left waiting
for a long time, as in 'When we got to town we
couldn't find anywhere to park, and the rest of them

went off shopping, leaving me in charge of the car,
twiddling my thumbs.' Certainly, people do tend unconsciously to play with their thumbs when they
find themselves idle, particularly when they are
waiting impatiently for something. Busy people,
who really cannot afford the time to be there, can
often be seeing making the gesture in doctors' waiting rooms.

The thumb and authority, dominance and aggression
The thumb has associations with authority. Someone in authority is said to 'give the thumbs down' to
a project if this has been rejected. If someone is
dominated by another person, we say that he or she
is 'under his or her thumb'.

Thus we find that the thumb in body language is often associated with dominance, superiority or authority, and even aggression. A teacher who tucks his hands round the sides of his gown, or the lapels of his jacket, and displays his raised thumb is subconsciously emphasising his position of superiority and dominance. The gesture, which sometimes involves only one hand and one thumb, is a favourite one with barristers in court, at least according to television series.

A gesture that involves hands deeply thrust in pockets, often trouser pockets, with the thumbs displayed can be a signal of dominance or superiority. It can also be a sign of aggression, as though the person making the gesture were issuing a challenge to the world. Thumbs protruding from pockets can also be a courtship, preening gesture, a kind of sexual come-on, as though it were proclaiming, 'Hey, look at me!'

Another gesture that involves the thumb also suggests these three signals of superiority, aggression and sexuality. It occurs when the thumbs are tucked into a belt or trouser waistband.

The lower part of the body also plays a part in body language. The hands-on-hips gesture has been mentioned above (*see* page 167) and has been dealt with in detail in the section on voluntary gestures (*see* page 93), but the hips have some significance on their own. They are frequently used in a kind of rolling movement as a kind of subconscious sexual come-on. This unconscious effort to attract a member of the opposite sex may also be accompanied by a pat of the hair or some other preening gesture. A more aggressive backup gesture is that of displaying the thumbs in trouser pockets, often the back pockets, or that of tucking the thumbs into a belt or waistband. These gestures are dealt with above in the comments on thumbs.

The legs

Crossing the legs

Just as some people cross their arms when subconsciously they wish to create a barrier between themselves and the people or situation around them, so some people cross their legs. If they are feeling particularly defensive they may well cross both their arms and their legs, although some women adopt such a position, particularly when sitting, to signal that they are very angry. If someone suddenly crosses the arms and legs it is as well to be on your guard because it is one of the signs that someone is lying. Look out for other signs.

If the arms are not crossed it is as well not to assume that the crossed legs indicate a defensive or negative attitude if the owner of the crossed legs is sitting down. People of both sexes sometimes cross their legs out of habit, or even just to get comfortable, especially if they are expecting to be sitting for some time. Indeed, many people when sitting for a long time cross and uncross their legs several times in an effort to acquire a reasonable degree of comfort. This crossing and uncrossing gesture can also indicate that the person who is sitting, possibly as part of an audience at a lecture, is rather bored by what is being said or by what is happening.

Women in particular often cross their legs automatically, some of them perhaps subconsciously remembering lessons learnt as children that it was ladylike to sit with one's legs crossed and totally unacceptable for women to sit with their legs apart. This would have been regarded as extremely immodest, especially in the days before it was common for women and girls to wear trousers. Unlike men, women also sometimes wrap one foot round the lower calf when they are sitting with crossed legs. This can be an indication that the woman is feeling defensive or ill at ease, since wrapping the foot round the leg is reinforcing the crossed-legs position.

Far from crossing their legs in a defensive attitude when they are seated, some women do so quite unconsciously, in such a way as to display their legs to best advantage, particularly if the said legs are encased in particularly attractive stockings or tights. The legs are neatly or elegantly crossed at the knees, usually right leg over left leg, and the legs are placed close together. This suggestion that the woman is unconsciously displaying her legs is enhanced if the woman keeps looking at her legs and, even more so, if she keeps touching her legs or stroking the thighs. She may also keep crossing and uncrossing her legs. Thus, crossed legs can be a preening gesture and an unconscious sexual come-on, as far as the female sex is concerned.

Crossing the ankles

A less sexual version of the 'sit like a lady' gesture is the sitting position that still involves the crossing of the legs but has the legs crossing at the ankles. This looks rather a prim gesture and can be a sign that the person, if female, is rather conventional in outlook. For example, British citizens are used to seeing their queen sitting in this way but not younger members of the royal family, who are more likely to cross their legs at the knee.

Crossing the ankles is not simply a signal of female conventionality or primness. Men, as well as women, use this gesture, and it is sometimes, more often in men than in women, a sign of a defensive or negative attitude. Indeed, it is more likely to be so than the gesture involving legs that are crossed at the knees, particularly if the ankles are crossed very tightly, as if to create a very tight barrier between the ankle-crosser

and the rest of the world. The style of ankle-crossing adopted by the male usually differs from that adopted by women. Women tend to keep their knees together while crossing the ankles, but men often have their knees open when their ankles are crossed.

Men are more likely than women to cross their legs at the knee for defensive or negative reasons, although it is as well to look out for other backup gestures to confirm this. A leg-cross gesture probably still more common among American males than among European males, and still uncommon in women, is that in which the ankle of one leg is brought to rest on top of the knee of the other leg. Such a gesture may be indicative of an argumentative or competitive personality or attitude. This interpretation of the gesture is more likely to be correct if the person crossing his knees has one or both hands on the top leg, as though locking it in position. This certainly reinforces the suggestion of an argumentative or stubborn personality.

Sitting with the legs apart

Unlike women, who have been taught to preserve their modesty, men often sit with their legs apart. If the legs are very wide apart it can be a sign that the person sitting in this way is a very arrogant and aggressive person. If there are women present it can be a signal that the male is drawing attention to his sexuality, and so the gesture can be construed as a sexual come-on or part of a rather macho courtship technique.

Sitting with the legs together

In theory, sitting with the legs together but not tightly clamped, should be a relaxed position, but it is one that few of us adopt unless we are in a situation that encourages this position – for example, if we are sitting behind a desk – or unless we are in a particularly formal situation and are more on our guard than usual. Particularly if the hands are folded in the lap, the position,

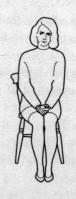

rather than relaxed, can look overly prim or self-conscious, as though the person was not at ease. Perhaps the position reminds us too much of sitting in rows at school having the class photograph taken.

Standing

All the leg positions described above have related to a sitting position, but legs also produce body signals when people are standing. If someone is standing with crossed legs this is much more likely to be an indication of a defensive or negative attitude than if the person with crossed legs is sitting down. This is particularly true if the arms are crossed as well, thereby creating a double barrier. You will often see people who are strangers to each other standing in such a way, for example at a bus stop. People who have just arrived at a party or function where they do not know anyone will often adopt such a stance until they get to know one of the other guests with whom they feel comfortable and so can relax. It is their unconscious way of indicating that they wish to keep their distance. The gesture could just indicate that the people concerned are cold, although this is less likely than if they are simply hugging themselves against the cold, and it could indicate that the person concerned wishes to go to the bathroom.

Legs locked together

It has been described above, under sitting positions, (*see* page 191) how some women wrap one foot around the calf of the other leg when sitting with crossed legs and how this can be an indication of a defensive attitude or feelings of unease. A similar position is adopted by some women when they are standing up. They subconsciously lock one foot around the lower part of the other leg, frequently holding on to a door or something, and this is very likely to be a signal that the person is defensive and ill at ease. The barrier against the world might not be so obvious as other barriers, but it is there.

Rubbing the foot of one leg up and down the back of the other
Another standing gesture that can suggest a lack of ease, and often distinct nervousness, is that of rubbing the foot of one leg up and down the back of the other leg. Again this is a gesture most likely to be made by women.

Legs wide apart
As has been indicated above, a man sitting with legs wide apart can signal aggression. Signs of aggression can also be transmitted by people adopting a similar pose when standing. Unlike the sitting position, such a pose can also be adopted by women, although their legs are not usually quite so far apart as those of men. An angry woman might well stand

with legs apart, and possibly also with arms akimbo, when encountering a husband very late home for dinner.

The legs wide apart gesture is also used by men in the presence of women as an unconscious indicator of their sexuality, and possibly also of their dominance. This is particularly likely to be the correct interpretation of the gesture if the man also has his thumbs tucked into his belt or has his hands tucked into his trouser pockets with thumbs displayed.

In a comfortable, relaxed standing position the legs are usually slightly apart. If they are very close together it tends to suggest that the person adopting the stance is very much subordinate to the person to whom he or she is talking or is being very respectful to him or her. The stance is reminiscent of a schoolboy respectfully listening to the headmaster.

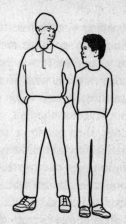

The feet

Feet can also give interesting body signals. Foot-tapping is the most obvious one of these. It is used to convey anger and impatience and, although it can be used quite unconsciously, it is often an intentional gesture and has been dealt with in the chapter on voluntary gestures (*see* page 95).

Some involuntary foot gestures have been described under leg gestures above. These include the locking of a foot round the other leg and the rubbing of a foot up and down the back of the other leg. Other foot signals are more subtle and can be a good indication of someone's attitude.

Pointing with the feet

Such foot gestures are often related to the direction in which the foot is pointing. If you are engaged in conversation with someone who, from their facial gestures, seems to be quite happy in your company but who has the feet, or a foot, pointing towards the door, then for some reason that person wants to be off. It may be that he or she is bored with the conversation or it may be that he or she has a pressing appointment elsewhere, but for whatever reason an exit is desired.

The above is true whether the person is sitting or standing. When people are standing talking to us we are not likely to look at what their feet or the lower part of their bodies are doing. If a person is sitting down it may be easier to deduce a true reaction from the direction in which his or her feet, or foot, points There may be other signs that an imminent departure is desired. For example, the person may lean forward with hands gripping the arms or sides of the chair, or may lean forward with hands on the knees, as though getting ready to rise.

The feet do not always give negative signals. They can be a sign of interest or attraction. For example, if a group of people at a meeting or function are standing talking, you will observe that the feet – either one or both – of the people who find each other interesting and wish to converse more have automatically turned to point towards each other. A similar phenomenon can be noticed when people are sitting down, and in this case crossed knees, as well as the feet, are pointed at the person whom the maker of the gesture is interested in or attracted to.

Seeing past the imprecision

Thus the whole body helps in the complex procedure of getting to grips with how people really are, rather than with how they would like to be. Body language is as yet rather an imprecise area of study, but it at least offers some guidelines as to how we should interpret the gestures of our fellow men and women, and gives us an insight into their personalities that we would not otherwise have had.

Involuntary gestures

Listed below, for ease of reference, are involuntary gestures that are dealt with in detail above. Others may be dealt with in the chapter on voluntary gestures and are simply referred to above.

head

head-nodding	indicating agreement or encouragement
head-shaking	indicating disagreement or discouragement
head tilt	indicating interest
lowering of head	indicating negative signals or indicating sadness or depression or indicating contemplation or indicating submission
head-tossing	indicating vanity or indicating a sexual come-on

head supported by hand
> indicating tiredness or boredom

head with clasped hands behind it
> indicating authority or superiority
> or indicating confidence

hair

hair-patting or hair-touching
> indicating vanity or indicating
> preening gesture as a sexual come-
> on or indicating discomfort

pushing back hair from forehead
> indicating preening gesture as a
> sexual come-on or indicating
> nervousness

pushing hair behind ears
> indicating nervousness or indicating
> preening gesture as sexual come-on

pushing hair off back of neck
> indicating nervousness

hair-twisting indicating nervousness

hair-sucking or hair-chewing
> indicating nervousness or indicat-
> ing concentration

brow

furrowed brow	indicating anger or indicating anxiety or worry or indicating puzzlement or indicating deep thought
hand to brow	indicating anxiety or worry or indicating tiredness or indicating pain or indicating deep thought or indicating attempts to remember
brow-slapping	indicating annoyance at having forgotten something.

eyebrows

eyebrow flashing	indicating friendly greeting or recognition.

eyes

eye expressions	indicating pleasure, amusement, anger, love, fear, etc
eye-widening	indicating surprise or shock
minimal eye contact	
	indicating dishonesty or indicating shyness or nervousness
eye-swerving	indicating boredom or indicating nervousness or indicating lying

eye-opening and eye-closing
        indicating nervousness

eye-touching	indicating nervousness or indicating doubt or uncertainty or indicating lying
eye-rubbing	indicating tiredness
staring	indicating dominance or authority or indicating day dreaming
closed eyes	indicating tiredness or indicating boredom or indicating exasperation or frustration
half-closed eyes	indicating passion or indicating anger or indicating concentration

peeping under eyelashes
        indicating modesty or shyness or indicating flirtatiousness

cheeks

cheek-touching	indicating evaluation or concentration or indicating anxiety

ears

touching or rubbing earlobe
        indicating nervousness or indicating doubt or indicating lying

screwing finger in earhole
> indicating a desire to shut out
> sound or noise or indicating a
> desire to shut out what is going on
> around one or indicating a signal
> that one wishes to speak

bending ear over earhole
> indicating a desire to shut out sound
> or noise or indicating a desire to shut
> out what is going on around one

rubbing of ear   indicating a desire to shut out
> sound or noise or indicating a
> desire to shut out what is going
> around us.

nose

nose-scratching, rubbing, touching
> indicating nervousness or indicat-
> ing doubt or indicating puzzlement
> or indicating lying

nose-rubbing   *see above* under *nose-scratching*

nose-touching   *see above* under *nose-scratching*

mouth

smiling   indicating happiness or pleasure

grimacing	indicating distaste or displeasure
open mouth	indicating surprise or shock
hand over mouth	indicating lying
fingers over mouth	
	indicating lying
fingers in mouth	indicating insecurity or indicating anxiety.

lips

lip-wetting	indicating sexual attraction or lasciviousness

tongue

tongue between teeth	
	indicating concentration
teeth-chewing	indicating tension or nervousness
clenched teeth	indicating an attempt to control anger
hair-chewing	indicating nervousness or indicating concentration
nail-biting	indicating nervousness or indicating insecurity

chin

chin-stroking	indicating deep thought or indicating admiration
chin-rubbing	indicating doubt
chin-touching	indicating nervousness or lying
chin cupped in hand	indicating deep thought
chin cupped in two hands	indicating low spirits or indicating deep thought
chin and jaw protruding	indicating aggression or indicating defensiveness or indicating determination
chin and jaw tucked into neck	indicating reticence or indicating lack of confidence

neck

sticking neck out and pulling it in again	indicating nervousness or anxiety
neck-touching	indicating nervousness or indicating lying or indicating doubt
neck-clasping	indicating anger

neck-scratching below ear lobe
    indicating doubt or uncertainty

neck-slapping   indicating a realisation that one has
    forgotten something

arms

arm-folding   indicating defensiveness or insecu-
    rity or indicating negative
    thoughts or indicating lying

arm-folding with clenched fists
    indicating defensiveness combined
    with hostility or indicating
    defensiveness combined with
    aggression

arm-folding with upturned thumbs
    indicating defensiveness combined
    with self-confidence

partial arm-folding
    indicating slight feelings of defen-
    siveness or insecurity or
    indicating slightly negative
    thoughts

arms at sides   indicating sense of ease

Body Language

arms behind back with hands clasped
> indicating sense of ease or indicating confidence or indicating authority

arms behind head indicating confidence or indicating arrogance

hands

hand-clasping indicating nervousness or insecurity

hands folded indicating state of relaxation or indicating conventionality or primness

hand-wringing indicating nervous tension or anxiety

clenched hands indicating tension or indicating an attempt to control emotions

hand-steepling, raised
> indicating superiority or authority or indicating evaluation or indicating positive response

hand-steepling, lowered
> indicating evaluation or indicating negative response or indicating doubt

hands pressed together with palms flat
> indicating emphasis or indicating attempt to persuade

hands clasped behind back
> indicating sense of ease or indicating confidence or indicating authority

hands folded behind head
> indicating confidence or indicating arrogance

hand on hip   indicating anger or indicating vanity or indicating sexual come-on

hand supporting chin
> indicating deep thought

two hands supporting chin
> indicating low spirits or indicating deep thought

open palm   indicating openness and honesty

fingers

jabbing finger   indicating emphasis or indicating dominance or authority

fingernail-biting   indicating nervousness

fingernail examination
indicating nervousness or indicating boredom

thumbs

thumb-twiddling   indicating idleness or indicating impatience

thumbs displayed with fingers tucked in lapels
indicating superiority or dominance

thumbs displayed with fingers tucked into trouser pocket   indicating dominance or superiority or indicating aggression or indicating a sexual come-on

thumbs tucked into belt or waistband
indicating dominance or superiority or indicating aggression or a sexual come-on.

hips

hand on hip   indicating anger or indicating vanity or a sexual come-on

rolling hips   indicating sexual come-on

legs

legs crossed at knee in sitting position
> indicating defensiveness or nega-
> tive thoughts or in women
> indicating conventional 'ladylike'
> position;

crossing and uncrossing legs
> indicating a desire to get comfort-
> able or in women indicating
> a sexual come-on;

legs crossed at ankle in sitting position with knees
together
> indicating in women conventional
> ladylike position, primness or
> conventionality.

legs crossed with one foot wrapped round other leg in
women
> indicating defensiveness or lack of
> ease

legs open in sitting position with ankles crossed in men
> indicating defensiveness or nega-
> tive thoughts

legs crossed in sitting position with the ankle of one
leg placed on top of knee in men
> indicating argumentative personal-
> ity or mood or competitive person-
> ality

legs wide apart in sitting position in men
> indicating arrogance or indicating
> aggression or as a sexual come-on

legs crossed in standing position
> indicating defensiveness or nega-
> tive thoughts or indicating coldness
> or indicating desire to go to the
> toilet

one leg with foot of other leg wrapped round it in

standing position in women
> indicating defensiveness or lack of
> ease

rubbing one foot against the back of the opposite leg
> indicating nervousness or lack of
> ease

legs wide apart in standing position
> indicating anger or indicating
> aggression or indicating sexual
> come-on

legs very slightly apart in standing position
> indicating a state of relaxation

legs placed very close together with heels together
> indicating subordinate position or
> indicating great respect

feet

foot wrapped round calf of other leg in sitting position
see above at leg

*foot wrapped round calf of other leg in standing
position* see above at leg

foot rubbing against the back of the other leg
see above at leg

foot or feet pointing to door or exit
indicating a wish to go away

foot or feet pointing towards someone
indicating an interest or feeling of
attraction towards that person

CHAPTER 4

Other Body Signals

There are several other elements in body language, as well as gestures or body movements, that can provide a key to someone's personality or mood. Again, as with some aspects of body language, some of these elements overlap with each other and with some gestures.

Posture

There is something to be learnt from the posture of people as well as from their body movements. Studying the posture of someone with whom you are to have some kind of dealings before you actually meet him or her can be very useful, since you can adjust your approach in the light of what you learn.

Erect posture

For example, people who stand up straight and have an erect bearing tend to be very confident individuals who have a good opinion of themselves and of their abilities and tend to be dominant personalities. Their posture signals authority and high status. If their posture is straight and erect to an exceptional, indeed to an unnatural degree, they can be very arrogant or overbearing, but it is just possible that they have been in military service for a long time, and their posture could simply be a part of their professional training.

Stooping posture

On the other hand, people who seem to droop and be all hunched up tend to have low self-esteem and have little confidence in themselves and their abilities. It is as if they are trying to hide themselves by slouching and sagging. The posture of such people signals submissiveness and low status.

Of course these are two extreme cases. Many people do not fit either of these but come somewhere in between. Nevertheless, it is worthwhile observing which of the two extremes someone tends towards, if you, for example, do business with him or her.

There are factors other than personality type that

affect posture. Some people are self-conscious about some attribute of their bodies, and this can subconsciously be reflected in their posture. For example, a young person who is exceptionally tall and both dislikes this unusual height and is embarrassed by it might unconsciously adopt a stooping posture to reduce his or height. Unfortunately, such a stoop of the head and shoulders is much more unattractive than exceptional height.

Similarly, an adolescent girl might unconsciously develop a shoulder hunch because she is embarrassed about developing large breasts. Again it is unfortunate that all she is doing is making herself less attractive by going around with a permanent shrug.

Profession affects posture

Occasionally someone's profession affects his or her posture. We have seen above how people in the armed services tend to have an exceptionally erect posture. On the other hand, people who spend their days at word processors or typewriters or in book study often end up with a decidedly hunched posture

Posture is dependent on mood

To some extent posture is dependent on mood as

well as on personality type. If someone is feeling very bright and happy, and generally feeling good about themselves, this is likely to show in his or her posture. He or she walks in a sprightly way, with his or her head held higher than usual, possibly with the arms swinging, and tends to take longer steps than usual – they are the picture of happiness.

If, however, people are feeling depressed this tends to be reflected in a more slouched, more bowed down, posture. The shoulders tend to sag and the head tends to droop. They look as though they are carrying the burdens of the world on their shoulders and are the very picture of misery.

Again, many people fall between these two extremes, but it is as well to observe how mood affects the posture of those around you. This could well be of benefit to you and stop you making a few mistakes yourself. For example, if you plan to ask the boss for a substantial rise you could figure out what for him or her is a buoyant mood and make your request, rather than risk almost certain refusal by asking during what you have learn to recognise as a black mood.

Posture when sitting
Much can be learnt about mood and general state of

mind from the posture of people and from the way they are standing or sitting. For example, someone who is slumped in a chair is likely to be experiencing some kind of negative feeling. He or she may be very tired, very bored or very uninterested, and be just waiting for the end of the working day to arrive. We have all at some time or other come home from work utterly exhausted and devoid of energy and slumped into the nearest armchair. This is the habitual position of what has become known as a couch potato, someone who takes very little exercise but watches television video most of the time, having little interest in anything else.

Thus, people who are slumped in chairs are tired or uninterested or overly relaxed. On the other hand people who are sitting on the very edge of their chairs are likely to be feeling very tense and totally unrelaxed. They tend to be people who are of a tense, nervous disposition generally or else be in a tense, nervous mood. Those occupants of a dentist's wait-

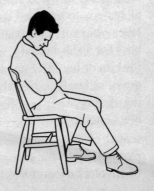

ing room who are absolutely terrified of dentists often sit like this, and in fact the kind of chair with which such waiting rooms are usually furnished lends itself more to this kind of sitting than to the relaxed slump.

Stance and sitting position are often related to body gestures, and these have been referred to under the relevant body part, mostly in the section on involuntary gestures. For example, we have seen in the comments on gestures and positions involving the legs that someone standing with legs very wide apart is likely to be in an angry or aggressive mood (*see* page 196). Similarly, we have seen that someone standing with crossed legs is likely to be feeling defensive and uneasy, particularly if the person has crossed arms as well (*see* page 195).

Seated positions, some of which have been dealt with above, also give clues to mood and personality. For example, a man sitting with one leg balanced on the knee of the other is likely to be of a competitive or argumentative disposition, whereas a woman sitting with legs crossed and with one foot locked round the calf of the other leg is likely to be feeling defensive and ill at ease. Again, these, and other seated positions, are dealt with in earlier chapters, particularly in the comments on legs in the chapter on involuntary gestures (*see* page 190).

Body Language

Sometimes people, particularly men, straddle chairs sitting with their faces towards the back and leaning on their arms, which are folded across the back of the chairs. This suggests that the chair-straddlers are aggressive and dominant people who are using the chair backs as a kind of shield or defence.

Walking pace

Walking pace differs from person to person, varying to some extent with the age of the person, with the health and state of fitness of the person and with the location of the person – people in large cities often walk much faster than people in small villages, perhaps because of the pace of life, perhaps because of the fear of crime. As a general rule, however, confident and happy people are more likely to adopt a brisk pace with a light and springy step, while people who are lacking in confidence and self-esteem and are feeling unhappy are more likely to adopt a slow, shuffling pace with a heavy, rather dragging step.

People who walk along with their hands in their pockets can possibly be feeling cold, if the temperature is low. In the absence of cold, however, we have to consider that the person with hands in pockets is feeling withdrawn in some way. If the person is also kicking any stones that get in the way, or is even kicking imaginary objects, then he or she is feeling either angry or is feeling dispirited or at a loose end, certainly not upbeat. His or her head is probably also bowed, although this can be a sign of deep thought.

Standing

Standing totally upright is very tiring and something that we therefore do not do all the time. Very often we lean on something. We lean against any vertical firm support that we can find – walls, doorposts, lampposts and so on, anything to take the weight off our feet, so to speak.

Leaning

What we lean on can sometimes be a guide to our attitude or feelings. Leaning can be an unconscious proprietorial gesture, as though we are establishing a territorial claim. For example, we might lean on the doorpost of our house when we are talking to a salesman on the doorstep with no intention of letting him in any further. It is as if we are saying, 'This is mine and you can't have it.'

Similarly, if we are in a group of people standing in a car park chatting, we may well find ourselves leaning against out respective cars, thereby unconsciously exercising ownership rights, except, perhaps if everyone else has an up market car and we have a rusty old banger that is on its last legs.

An extension of this kind of leaning occurs when someone sitting behind an office desk puts a foot on it. Once again, he is doing this subconsciously to establish territorial rights. Such an action sometimes takes place when a person who makes the owner of the office desk feel threatened in some way has entered the office or is standing by the desk. By putting his feet on the desk, the occupant of the office can really be indicating that he is establishing his right not only to the desk but to his place in the firm.

Sometimes this unconscious proprietorial leaning extends to people as well as to things. You may see a man leaning against his partner, or indeed a woman leaning against her partner, at a party or meeting where there is a large group of people. This is particularly likely to happen if the said group contains some unattached people, especially physically attractive people. Someone leaning against a partner in such a situation is subconsciously saying, 'He/she is mine. Keep off!'

Ownership claims on people do not necessarily involve actual leaning. These can also take the form of putting one's arm around someone or taking someone's elbow or hand in one's own hand. The message is the same.

Leaning against someone or something does not necessarily indicate subconscious ownership rights. Indeed, it can be an attempt to challenge these and make the owner of the relevant object or the partner of the relevant person feel intimidated or threatened.

Thus, someone who is sitting in someone else's office and suddenly puts his feet on the desk, unless he is an extremely good friend and is behaving in an exceptionally relaxed way, may subconsciously be trying to intimidate the occupant of the office by challenging his right to the desk. A similar situation can occur if someone is leaning on the door or doorpost of someone else's office.

Unconsciously making someone feel threatened by making proprietorial gestures – unwittingly or otherwise – is not restricted to places and objects. It extends to people. For example, an unattached man at a party may put his arm around someone else's partner to lead her to the place where food and drink is being served or to introduce her to someone else in the room. Her partner may well feel threatened, irrespective of the intentions of the other male.

Similarly, an unattached female may make a corresponding gesture to another woman's partner with the same resultant feelings in the partner.

Leaning against something may have another subconscious motive, other than establishing proprietorial rights or intimidation. It may indicate a subconscious desire to protect oneself. Thus, if you are in a lift or elevator with only one other person you might lean against the back of the lift subconsciously to protect your back and keep the potential enemy in sight. Similarly, if you are standing at a bus stop you might lean against the back of the bus shelter or against the pole indicating the bus stop.

If you have just met someone and realise that he or she is leaning slightly towards you then the likelihood is that he or she is feeling kindly disposed towards you and is in a friendly mood. On the other hand, if the person is leaning slightly away from you then the likelihood is that he or she is feeling some degree of hostility towards you and is in an unfriendly mood.

Lying down

The position that we adopt when lying down also tells something about us. Of course, fewer people will glean information from our recumbent position than will glean it from our standing or sitting position since lying down is a more private matter, conducted in front of relatively few people.

Sleeping positions

If we regularly sleep in a tight foetal position, with the body tightly curled up into a ball, the knees drawn up towards the chest and the arms hugging the body, we tend to be rather insecure people. We are subconsciously seeking the safety and protection that we experienced pre-birth in our mothers' wombs.

A slightly less tight, more relaxed form of the foetal position, called the semi-foetal position, is one of the most common sleeping positions. The sleeper in this position has the knees and arms in the same position as in the foetal position but they are loosely, not

tightly, bent. The looser position allows the sleeper to turn more easily. Unlike the tight foetal position, the more relaxed semi-foetal position does not suggest deep insecurity but indicates a life of reasonable equanimity.

People who regularly lie flat on their backs with limbs flung wide are apt to be people who are confident, secure and completely open. They unconsciously feel not at all threatened and so do not need to protect themselves.

On the other hand, people who regularly lie face down with arms and legs stretched out tend to be people who feel the need to control their lives completely. By adopting such a position they are taking up a great deal of space while at the same time protecting the most important part of themselves, as though they unconsciously feel in some way under threat.

Spatial zones

An important part of nonverbal communication relates to space. When two people meet for the first time the ideal amount of space between them is that which allows them to be close enough to show their interest in each other but not so close as to make either of them feel oppressed.

Four boundaries or zones have been identified and categorised in our spatial relationship to each other.

The intimate zone

The zone that relates to people that have a very close relationship with each other extends roughly from 0 to 50 centimetres. People who are allowed to come within this range, called the intimate zone, include husbands and wives, partners and lovers, children and parents, close family members, such as brothers and sisters, and close friends. Only the members of this group closest to the person involved would be allowed within the inner part of  this range, roughly up to about 15 to 18 centimetres. Sometimes other people come within the intimate zone in some professional capacity, people who cannot do their jobs if they cannot achieve entrance to this space. Such people include doctors, dentists or hairdressers.

The personal zone

The next closest zone to the intimate zone is called the personal zone and extends roughly from 50 centimetres to 1.25 metres. This is the spatial zone occupied by people at social gatherings, such as drinks parties. This distance allows peo-

ple who do not know each other well – perhaps they have just been introduced – to converse comfortably and get to know each other without feeling threatened by over-closeness.

The social zone

The zone one further out from the personal zone is called the social zone, and it extends roughly from 1.25 metres to 4 metres. This is the zone that is usually occupied by strangers with whom we come into contact, sometimes regular contact, in the course of our day-to-day lives. These people include workmen doing work around the house, local shopkeepers, the postman, the milkman, the local policeman, and so on.

The public zone

The fourth and furthest zone is called the public zone, a distance roughly over 4 metres from the person involved. People who are listening to a public lecture, for example, are this far away and more from the lecturer. Similarly, the members of an audience are placed at such a distance from the actors in a performance on stage.

Some people tolerate other people's closeness more than others. Nevertheless, all of us tend to ob-

ject to, and resent, the entry of people who are not close friends or relatives, or professionals such as doctors, into our intimate zone. There is a subconscious fear that anyone else who enters it is an intruder who feels hostile to us and is planning an attack of some kind, sometimes an unwanted sexual advance.

Violation of the zones

When someone enters our intimate zone certain physiological changes occur in our bodies. Our adrenaline levels increase markedly, our hearts beat faster, and more blood is pumped to the brain. This is an indication that the body of the person whose space has been invaded is preparing itself for action. The action may take the form of sexual passion if the person entering the intimate zone is a lover, but it may take the form of some kind of hostile attack or rebuff, or of flight, if the person is an intruding stranger.

When we meet people for the first time we should be careful not to invade their intimate space. This is particularly true of people who tend to be of an exceptionally informal, over-friendly disposition, hail-fellow-well-met types who put their arms round the shoulders of others on the slightest acqaintanceship. They are tactile people themselves, but they should remember that many other people are not, and that such people will resent undue physical contact with a stranger. If the person making the overly friendly gesture is a salesman putting his arm round the shoulder of a potential customer who is a complete stranger, then he is likely to lose the sale.

Sometimes encroaching on another's intimate zone is quite unavoidable. If, for example, people are standing in a crowded bus or train they are unlikely to be able to preserve either their intimate zones or those of their neighbours, since space is so limited. But those really intent on preserving as much of their personal territory as possible and totally dedicated to repelling any stranger's attempt to invade this find ways to make this clear.

Such a person will avoid making eye contact with

anyone else in case he or she takes it as an overture to a conversation. He or she will try not to betray any emotion, even if someone steps on a foot, as that would admit the existence of someone else in the precious intimate zone. Often people who wish to preserve the sanctity of their territory will hide themselves behind a book or newspaper, whether or not they are actually reading it, if they find themselves in a crowded place. If they have neither book nor paper, they may well examine any piece of writing or illustration that is present. Advertisements on a bus or the different routes indicated on underground trains are cases in point, as are the numbers of the floors listed on the control panel of a lift. The personal stereo might have been expressly designed to preserve the privacy of the intimate zone as it gives everyone a legitimate reason for switching off from the people around them.

As has been indicated above, the zone that separates people who do not know each other well at drinks parties is known as the personal zone. Since parties are a favourite place for unattached people to get to know each other and perhaps form close relationships, it is very likely that someone will unconsciously break the unwritten zone law if he or she is attracted to someone at the party. People in such a situation may unconsciously move forwards, leaning forwards as they do. If this forward movement is not acceptable to the person who is the object of attraction, he or she is likely first to lean back and then, if the forward movement goes on, to step backwards. In this way the personal zone is unconsciously preserved.

Members of audiences or spectators are often disconcerted if the public zone is breached. This can happen if a comedian or singer who is giving a stage performance suddenly makes an unscheduled leap from the stage into the audience and goes on with the act from there. Even if the performer does not invite a member of the audience to join in – an invitation guaranteed to cause acute embarrassment to all but the most outgoing of people – there is a general feeling of uneasiness among the audience as their territory has been invaded.

Seating arrangements

Something can be learnt about people from the position they occupy at a table. A round table is the most democratic shape of table. Each person seated at it has an equal amount of territory, and there is no obviously dominant position at it. Because of this, a round table is more likely to promote a relaxed discussion among the people who are sitting at it.

The round table is, of course, really democratic only when the people around it are of more or less equal status. If an office meeting is taking place at a round table and the head of department or managing director is present, where he or she is sitting will unconsciously be deemed to be the head of the table, although this seems a contradiction in terms with reference to a round table. King Arthur is said to have had a round table so that all his knights would be of equal status, but this was slightly naive since whoever was sitting next to him at any given time would subconsciously take some kind of precedence over the others because of his physical proximity to the king.

The pecking order is more clearly demonstrated at a rectangular or oblong table. Here there is very little possibility of equality of status, at least for the duration of a meeting around such a table. The person who sits at the end of the table away from the door will automatically be assumed to be in charge, and of course it is the position that the head of department, managing director, chairman of the board, etc, will occupy. He or she is in a position to look down the table at everyone else, and with the back to the room subconsciously feels free from threat and attack.

Some people believe that where people sit at meetings at a rectangular table affects the amount of power that they will wield. Thus, at meetings where there is likely to be some form of power struggle or

political machinations, efforts may be made to rig the seating with a view to influencing the outcome of the meeting.

There is, however, some dispute among people as to which member of the group is first in importance after the person at the head of the table. Many would opt for the person who is seated to the right of the person at the head of the table. The feeling is that this person is number two in the power base and is a great supporter of the leader. As if to back up this assumption, we have the figurative phrase in the language 'right-hand man', or now also 'right-hand woman', which indicates someone who helps and supports, and is generally indispensable to, someone else who is in a position of power or responsibility.

Some people would argue that the person who is seated at the other end of the table, directly opposite the person in charge, is the least important. This person can be regarded as the bottom of the heap, being the furthest away from the most important person in the room, and so the most lacking in power and influence. However, to some extent this depends on the personality of the person at the foot of the table and on the situation.

The person sitting opposite the person in charge of the meeting is in a good position to be confrontational and issue challenges, making the bottom of the table a good place to sit if you are a very strong, competitive person who wishes to usurp the power of those at the head of the table.

If the person at the foot of the table is such a person, and if there is some kind of power struggle being waged, then the position at the foot of the table, far from being a humble one, can be an extremely important and pivotal one. The person at the right-hand side of the leader of the meeting is next in importance to the leader, simply because he or she is valuable to the leader. If the leader is losing power because of a political struggle, the person sitting directly opposite is quite likely to be the one who will acquire the lost power and quite likely to be the one who has engineered the power struggle.

At a small square or rectangular table in a bar, restaurant, office, etc., is the most friendly, cooperative position for two people to adopt is one sitting next to each other. This position is exceptionally suitable for people who are very good friends and are having a good old gossip, or for people who are working on a task together where the parameters have already been laid down and there is no real need for or possibility of competition. Especially if the cooperation is of a business nature the two chairs should not be so close together as to represent a threat to each other's territories. Apart from this restriction, the side-by-side position suggests an atmosphere of mutual trust and support, the implication being that you do not need to be in such a position that you have to keep a careful eye on each other.

Another quite friendly position that two people can adopt when sitting at a square or rectangular table is the corner or diagonal position. Such a position allows similar closeness to that of the sitting together position, but it does provide enough of a barrier for people to feel protected and unthreatened by excessive closeness. In a position of closeness without any barrier, some people feel threatened and defensive and so the corner or diagonal position is the perfect one for a relaxed, friendly interview.

When two people sit across a rectangular or square table from each other there can be an atmosphere of defensiveness or competitiveness. Often the table acts as a barrier, which emphasises the disagreement between them, and is more likely to lead to confrontation then to cooperation.

When someone in a position of power wishes to speak formally to a person in a more subordinate position, the meeting often takes place across a table. Again